PRO MEN ADE

... THROUGH THE PRESENT FUTURE

CITY OF CULTURE OF GALICIA

WITH ESSAYS BY
Maxwell L. Anderson, Lawrence Chua,
Rachel Healy, Ismail Serageldin,
Ramón Villares

AND PHOTOGRAPHS BY
Candida Höfer

XUNTA
DE GALICIA

fundación cidade
da cultura de galicia

SKIRA

Edited by
FOUNDATION FOR THE CITY OF
CULTURE OF GALICIA
Rúa de San Roque 2
Hospital de San Roque
E–15704 Santiago de Compostela
Tel. +34 881 997 565
Fax. +34 881 997 577
www.cidadeddacultura.org

Published by
SKIRA EDITORE
Palazzo Casati Stampa
Via Torino 61
I–20123 Milán
Tel. +39 02 724441
Fax. +39 02 72444211
www.skira.net

Project Management
A&M

Essays
Maxwell L. Anderson
Lawrence Chua
Rachel Healy
Ismail Serageldin
Ramón Villares

Translations
Carlos Mayor
Fernando Pazó
Esther Tallada
Josephine Watson

Design & Layout
trespuntos

Production Management
Elena Gaiardelli

Printed and bound in Italy. First edition.

ISBN 978-88-572-0643-1 (Skira editore)
ISBN 978-84-453-4990-8 (Xunta de Galicia)

Distributed in USA, Canada, Central & South America by Rizzoli International Publications, Inc., 300 Park Avenue South, New York, NY 10010, USA.
Distributed elsewhere in the world by Thames and Hudson Ltd., 181A High Holborn, London WC1V 7QX, United Kingdom.

Alberto Núñez Feijóo

President of Xunta de Galicia

For some time now towns have ceased to be merely "*urbs*"—urban forms or "city stones"—whose locations were chosen for practical reasons related to the need for settlements, shelter, relationships and bartering. For some time now they have been intense living organisms whose hearts we can examine, "*civitas*" that designate emotions, rituals and convictions that allude directly to the action of the men who transform them. Whether we be their technicians or their poets, their inhabitants or their painters, champions or critics, cities rise before us as constructions based on hopes and ideas rather than stone and concrete.

It is men who give them their meaning, who make them habitable and destroy them. They are the places in which we become more human and at once lose our humanity, complex fabrics of social hybridisation where we feel, think, dream, create—in short, where we live. Places inhabited by many; communal territories through which our discourses flow but also the cores of such discourses. Cities are not characterised by singularity but by diversity; they belong to everyone and in their uniqueness they embrace multiple pluralities. In their turn, they provide us with material organisations that act as the stage on which we play out our lives, which are re-contextualised moment by moment.

Atop the hill, the town waits for us, for all that energy that she will transform into culture, for the inert matter she will turn into living symbols of art, for all that which will finally end up giving her the name "city." In the meantime, *Promenade … Through the Present Future* invites you to begin a stroll on which you will be able to explore and become imbued with the dynamics of the city's possibilities and impossibilities, to understand and assume its disappointments in order to take your stance and contribute to raise its potential and reinvent it with unprecedented discoveries and setbacks. The fact is that only our invasive wandering will show us new solutions and ambitions for the city in the context of a new age, new relations, new professions, new knowledge and new values.

Roberto Varela Fariña

Minister for Culture and Tourism

Anthony Royal, the strange architect in James Graham Ballard's futuristic novel *High Rise*, tells us that cities were born with man and grew to protect and defend him from the threatening demons in the outside world. This explains why they were once encircled by walls, becoming impassable fortresses that safeguarded the hearts of men, their lives and their faith. Inside these walls we began to make up stories that developed on a par with houses and buildings and that not only obliged us to think of the city in terms of the need for rules and order, but as a cultural construction forged in the greatest power that belongs to us alone: that of dreaming up fictions that bring together memories, encounters and imaginaries through which we may live the various different lives we would have liked to lead when all we really have is one.

Biblical Babel, the besieged city in *The Iliad*, the *polis* in *The Eumenides*, the Baghdad in *The Thousand and One Nights* and "a place" in La Mancha in *Don Quixote*, Dickens' visions of London, the Paris described by Balzac, Baudelaire, Victor Hugo and Zola, the Berne through which Robert Walser "strolled" to the point of dementia to appease his anxiety and fill the days of his life, the Lisbon captured by Fernando Pessoa (or Álvaro de Campos, Ricardo Reis, Alberto Caeiro or Bernardo Soares), the Buenos Aires related by Borges and Cortázar, the Santiago de Compostela portrayed by Torrente Ballester, the Barcelona we discover in Eduardo Mendoza, the Madrid characterised by Javier Marías, the New York depicted by Paul Auster and the Shanghai represented by Neal Stephenson... The fact is that the city has always been literature, an open and endless text, a book (by Max Aub), "that is read as we walk, that is read with the feet," one which we overwrite or rewrite at each step with a new sensitivity.

With *Promenade ... Through the Present Future* the Ministry for Culture and Tourism of Xunta de Galicia invites strollers to write a new book and invites readers to amble through a new city that is more than a reality resulting from chance, design, time and memory. It is a city that exists because we imagine it, a city that faces up to the aggression or the invasion of the senses; a city of fantasy and frustration, freedom of rhetoric; a city that as a product of history and wakefulness we are still able to build, over and over, in order to make it into the place where our desires and expectations can circulate freely—the place it may already be.

INVISIBLE CITIES

CITIES & THE SKY 3

Those who arrive at Thekla can see little of the city, beyond the plank fences, the sackcloth screens, the scaffoldings, the metal armatures, the wooden catwalks hanging from ropes or supported by sawhorses, the ladders, the trestles. If you ask "Why is Thekla's construction taking such a long time?" the inhabitants continue hoisting sacks, lowering leaded strings, moving long brushes up and down, as they answer, "So that its destruction cannot begin." And if asked whether they fear that, once the scaffoldings are removed, the city may begin to crumble and fall to pieces, they add hastily, in a whisper, "Not only the city."

If, dissatisfied with the answers, someone puts his eye to a crack in a fence, he sees cranes pulling up other cranes, scaffoldings that embrace other scaffoldings, beams that prop up other beams. "What meaning does your construction have?" he asks. "What is the aim of a city under construction unless it is a city? Where is the plan you are following, the blueprint?"

"We will show it to you as soon as the working day is over; we cannot interrupt our work now," they answer.

Work stops at sunset. Darkness falls over the building site. The sky is filled with stars. "There is the blueprint," they say.

Contents

The End of the World as We Know It

Spatial Networks, Religion and Violence

Lawrence Chua

Pilgrimage sites were not only stage sets for religious rituals but were also theatres for mass violence and competing interpretations of political power. This essay uses case studies drawn from European and Southeast Asian architecture to show how historic pilgrimage networks revolved around such potent sites. The great circulation of pilgrims physically altered both the landscape and the architecture of religious sites. Diverse sites the Cathedral of Santiago de Compostela and Angkor Wat at the north of Siem Reap, made cosmological ideals present in the daily lives of people. Both the cathedral and the wat were the residence of an ecclesiastical power that transcended the earthly power of feudal lords and polities but was just as real as the centres of political power where kings held court. The moral communities that formed along pilgrimage networks were not necessarily related to communities existing under parochial, secular conditions and brought with them their own political agency that was sometimes independent of the intentions of royal, state and ecclesiastical power.

1 Santiago de Compostela.
1999

2 Angkor Wat, Siem Reap.
12th century

THE ARCHITECTURE OF THE ROMANESQUE period was the architecture of the end of the world. The twelfth century in Europe was a transitional political and economic period as dynasties came to an end and the balance of world power shifted. It was a time of mass veneration of the relics of saints but it was also a moment during which many Europeans anticipated the end of the world. The end of the world implied both a temporal and spatial ending. The important sites of this period, like the Cathedral of Santiago de Compostela, were not merely markers of physical borders in the temporal world, they also made tangible a particular understanding of the universe by incorporating users into their architectural rhythms. Pilgrimage routes like the Way of Saint James as well as those in non-European contexts were a form of creating shared or public space that brought pilgrims out of their parochial, local domains and united them into a new "moral" public. In this essay I will look at examples drawn largely from European and Southeast Asian sites to show how historic pilgrimage networks revolved around potent sites that were not only stage sets for religious rituals but also theatres for mass violence and competing interpretations of political power. While this argument can be extended to other religious contexts, historical conditions and regions, a full examination of pilgrimage sites across all religious and regional contexts is well beyond the scope of this brief essay.

THE FAR NORTHWESTERN TIP OF Spain at that time was considered to be the end of the earth. The centre of the known Christian world lay in cities like Rome and Jerusalem. The first crusade conquered Jerusalem in 1099. Nearly a century earlier, in 997 Santiago had been sacked by Muslim general Almanzor. The general made off with the cathedral's bells but was careful not to desecrate the actual tomb of Saint James. The bells were incorporated into the Great Mosque at Cordoba. The town, meanwhile, soon recovered and a new cathedral rose on the ruins of the old one. Though a few pilgrims to Santiago are recorded in the tenth century, it was in the early twelfth century that Santiago de Compostela came to rank with Rome and Jerusalem as one of the great destinations of mediaeval Christian pilgrimage. The first cathedral was built on top of the site of the tomb, and Benedictine houses were established along the developing pilgrimage route by monks from Cluny in Burgundy and from Aurillac in Cantal. This route was part of a larger political programme that was taking place on the Iberian Peninsula. By 1130, half of the peninsula had been conquered by kingdoms that claimed Christianity as their primary ideology.[1]

15

---

1 The nearly 800-year period of the Reconquest was complex and did not always fall into the conventional Christian *versus* Muslim narrative. Alliances across lines of faith were not uncommon. See Derek William Lomax, *The Reconquest of Spain* (New York: Prentice Hall, 1978), and María Rosa Menocal, *The Ornament of the World: How Muslims, Jews, and Christians Created a Culture of Tolerance in Medieval Spain* (Boston & New York: Back Bay Books/Little & Brown and Company, 2002).

3

4

5

A balance of power between ecclesiastical, economic and political actors was created through these new networks of pilgrimage. Pilgrims travelled en masse to the new cathedral along routes that cut through the central and southern parts of France before converging into one main road to Santiago de Compostela. These pilgrims set religious rituals like prayer, penance and thanksgiving in a network of roads, hospices and other services that led from four different towns: Saint-Denis or Chartres, Vézelay, Le Puy and Arles.[2] These networks were conduits for many things—first and foremost for pilgrims who sought a better life, whether through the acquisition of meaning, faith, romance or adventure, or simply to assuage loneliness.[3] These mobile communities were heterogeneous communities of people who came from different regions and classes within Europe. Most Europeans during this period were serfs and had to obtain permission from their feudal lords to leave their work behind. Feudal lords were more prone to grant permission to serfs who had outlived their usefulness to the feudal economy.

This great circulation of people physically altered both the landscape and the architecture of religious sites. The European landscape was transformed as an entire network of roads and hospices developed to support the pilgrims who had heard stories of miracles wrought by the relics of Saint James. As monks accommodated these pilgrims by modifying the basilican church plan to include an ambulatory, not only the physical characteristics of the church were transformed, so was the schedule of religious ritual itself. These ambulatories worked as an extension of the aisles to provide a continuous passageway around the entire church. Radiating chapels opened off the ambulatory. Additional chapels were sometimes built on the east side of the transepts for use by monks. These chapel altars could be visited by pilgrims without interrupting monastic services that were being conducted in the choir.

These sites made cosmological ideals present in the daily lives of people. The cathedral was the residence of an ecclesiastical power that transcended the earthly power of feudal lords and polities but was just as real as the centres of political power where kings held court. The moral communities that formed along these networks were not necessarily related to communities that exist under parochial, secular conditions. Pilgrims of different political backgrounds shared a common identity that transcended geographic and social origins. *Hajjis*, for instance, form a part of a Muslim *umma* that, ideally, transcends race and nationality. Anthropologists like Dean MacCannel and Erik Cohen consider modernity the transformative event in the development from

2   David Watkin, *A History of Western Architecture* (London: Laurence King, 1986), 134.
3   Chris Lowney, *A Vanished World: Medieval Spain's Golden Age of Enlightenment* (New York: Free Press, 2005), 84.

6

7

6 Mount Meru, Tibet. 2006

7 Towers of Angkor
Wat, Siem Reap. Gervais
Courtellemont, 1928

pilgrimage to tourism.[4] In Cohen's view, secularisation has robbed pilgrimage of much symbolic significance and mystical power and transformed its *loci* into attractions or mere destinations. Although Cohen's analysis hinges on an assumption of essential differences between "modern" and "traditional" states, he does point out that "traditional" societies were organised around a sacred centre that was the meeting point of the heavenly and earthly plane.[5] Perhaps a more accurate way of describing this and of developing a more historically nuanced understanding of how pilgrimage differs from tourism is to say that such centres are the confluence of two different forms of knowledge about place: a mundane and secular understanding of place and a sacred understanding of space. These different forms of knowledge existed in the same temporal moment and may even arise on the same journey.

19

A DRAMATIC EXAMPLE OF THIS are the Khmer temple complexes like Angkor Wat (*c.* twelfth century AD) that dot mainland Southeast Asia. Eleanor Mannikka's detailed study of the Angkor Wat complex reveals a site which was organised to align with the Hindu conception of the universe, both in theory and in lived reality. The centre of the complex is modelled on Mount Meru, the main foundational and vertical axis of the Hindu universe, and was built to incorporate astronomical rhythms and phases. In the fourteenth century, the king of the nearby polity of Sukhothai drew on these cosmological beliefs when he composed the *Traiphum Phra Ruang* [Three Worlds of Phra Ruang] from over thirty Buddhist doctrines.[6] The Traiphum is considered the first Thai Buddhist literary work of the Sukhothai period and is said to have been derived from Buddhist teachings but also to incorporate secular attitudes about righteousness, justice and other virtues.[7] The *Traiphum* organised the cosmos into thirty-one domains across three planes of existence: the Sensuous Plane or *Kamabhumi* [กามภูมิ], the Corporeal Plane or *Rupabhumi* [รูปภูมิ] and the Incorporeal Plane or *Arupabhumi* [อรูปภูมิ]. The human domain was located in the Sensuous Plane.

IN MANUSCRIPT DRAWINGS OF THE *Traiphum* artists have indicated the sacred universe with the markers of the known world. Certain trees that may have been familiar to local rulers were labelled within the realm of various planes of existence.[8] The *Traiphum*

---

4   Erik Cohen, "Pilgrimage and Tourism: Convergence and Divergence," in *Sacred Journeys: the Anthropology of Pilgrimage.* Alan Morris, ed. (Santa Barbara: Greenwood Press, 1992), 59.

5   *Ibidem*, 51.

6   The *Traiphum Phra Ruang* is said to have been composed by Phaya Lithai in 1345 AD. Namphueng Padamalangula, "Framing the Universe: Cosmography and the 'Discourse on the Frame' in *Traiphum Phra Ruang." Rian Thai. International Journal of Thai Studies,* vol. 1 n. 1 (Bangkok: Chulalongkorn University, 2008): 72.

7   King Lithai, *Traibhumikhatha: The Story of the Three Planes of Existence.* Thai National Team, trans. (Bangkok: Amarin Printing Group, 1987), 13.

8   See Henry Ginsburg, *Thai Manuscript Paintings* (London: British Library, 1988).

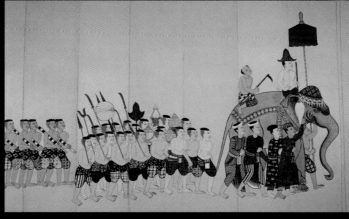

8 Mural paintings in Wat Ko Keo Suttharam depicting the various levels of Mount Meru, Phetchaburi. 1730

9 *Buddhist Holy Men*. Mincho, 1386

10 *The Pilgrimage to Sarabury* [detail]. 12th century

had an enormous influence on the world view of Siamese society and also had an important influence on planning, symbolism and ornamentation in architecture. The crematorium at royal *wat*, for instance, was organised according to this logic and royal cremation pyres are known as *merumaat* or *meruthong*.

AS SOUTHEAST ASIAN POLITIES IN the region developed into colonies and nation states with more clearly demarcated borders, tourism assumed a more prominent role than pilgrimage. Unlike pilgrimage, tourism was more often aimed at a national body, whether to underscore the importance of patrimony to an emerging national public or to sell exoticism to those who were "foreign." The nineteenth-century colonial archaeological projects at Angkor Wat, for instance, were intertwined with tourism. They allowed the French protectorate of Cambodia to pass as the gatekeeper of tradition by incorporating ancient, sacred spaces into the colonial map.[9] Complex economies emerged around many pilgrimage sites that are comparable to the industries that develop at major tourist destinations, although it would be inaccurate to say that they are the same.

THE ECONOMY OF PILGRIMAGE IS related more to the "moral economy of the poor" than to an exchange of goods and services. Edward Palmer Thompson describes this moral economy as focusing on a view of the proper economic functions of different parties within the community in eighteenth-century Europe.[10] The "moral economy of the poor" that Thompson described was related to social protest and suggests that there are some potentially radical differences between the types of community that pilgrims form and those formed by tourists. Pilgrims "belong" to the destination and are part of its ambience in a way that tourists are not. In the words of a French tourist, "A place is not good for tourists if it is too touristic."[11] Another key difference between "modern" travel and "traditional" pilgrimage revolves around absence and presence. In his engaging study of the Yemeni diaspora, Engseng Ho notes that before modernism, experiences of mobility involved complex and subtle interplays between absence and presence in many dimensions: tactile, visual, auditory, affective, aesthetic, textual and mystical.[12] Modern mobility, by contrast, seeks to be everywhere at once. It ignores absence and has difficulty recognising ways of affecting presence that take time. For Gananath Obeyesekere, Theravada Buddhist pilgrimage removes pilgrims from

---

9   Penny Edwards, *Cambodge: the Cultivation of a Nation, 1860–1945* (Honolulu: University of Hawai'i Press, 2007), 137.

10   Stanley J. Tambiah, *Buddhism and the Spirit Cults in North-east Thailand* (Cambridge: Cambridge University Press, 1970), 312.

11   *Ibidem* note 4, 58.

12   Engseng Ho, *The Graves of Tarim* (Berkeley: University of California Press, 2006), 10.

11 *Cambodge Angkor*
[advertising poster].
Jos Henri Ponchin, 1931

their parochial, local domains and unites them in an integrated "moral community" although they view pilgrimage in terms of their own particular religious or political interests.[13] While tourist travel may claim to remove its participants from their everyday contexts, it also removes them from the new local context to which they travel.

I   Pilgrimage and Public Space

THE "MORAL COMMUNITY" INTO WHICH pilgrims are integrated, while distinct from sedentary village and urban life, is a public space that is characterised by a reorganisation of relations among pilgrims and those who assist them on their journey to or at the shrine. These are not necessarily utopian communities: the residues of everyday social structure and hierarchy still remain. In Theravadan Buddhist pilgrimages, designations of status with regard to merit are apparent during the mass circumambulation of the *stupa* that takes place during festivals. The pilgrimage, as an act of merit-making that is produced in the public eye, is a way of demarcating public space. When these rituals happen in a space that conforms to a cosmological world view like the *Traiphum* or the basilican plan of a cathedral, it naturalises certain beliefs about hierarchy. Social hierarchies turn into celestial hierarchies or hierarchies with celestial mandates.

PILGRIMAGE SITES EMERGE AROUND BOTH relics and the personalities of the political figures who build the sites. The pilgrimage site is a sacred complex that visually represents narratives and symbols. The transfer and incorporation of sacred power, ritual and administrative links with secular, national authorities all contribute to the development of a pilgrimage centre. In Thailand, while a pilgrimage site often houses relics of the Buddha or other men of distinction, the real attraction of the place is the presence of the monk whose imagination and reputation were crucial to its development.[14] The monk, then, is a kind of "designer" of the pilgrimage site and plays an active role in defining it as a public space.

TRAVEL AWARDS PLACE, OR LOCATION, an important role in the reproduction of knowledge in a networked civilisation. In the Thai context, it was part of a process of creating distinctions between up-country Siam and Bangkok. Thongchai Winichakul writes

---

13   James B. Pruess, "Sanctification Overland: the Creation of a Thai Buddhist Pilgrimage Center," in *Sacred Journeys: the Anthropology of Pilgrimage … op. cit.,* 228.

14   *Idem,* "Merit-Seeking in Public: Buddhist Pilgrimage in Northeastern Thailand," *The Journal of the Siam Society,* vol. 64 n. 1. (Bangkok: The Siam Society, 1976): 225.

13

12 Buddhist monks at the Angkor Wat temples, Siem Reap. 2001

13 Buddhist monk in pilgrimage to Angkor Wat, Siem Reap. 2009

that travel was an instrument used by the Siamese elite to consolidate an ethnographic hierarchy between Siamese subjects spatially within the geo-body of Siam in relation to the superior space of Bangkok.[15] Travel before the late nineteenth century was not a desirable activity; political and social constraints as well as dangerous travelling conditions made it less enjoyable. Only traders and monks had the liberty to travel. Religious pilgrimages were primarily for acquiring inward wisdom and spiritual enlightenment. Wilderness was an ideal site for the search for wisdom because it was the negation of normal life, not because of any perceived aesthetic value: it was wild and adversarial and was to be subdued by the power of merit.[16] Siam lacked a discourse of the picturesque—a romantic view of nature—until the nineteenth century. It was during this period that there was a change in literary forms, economy and technology. Thongchai points to the transformation of the *nirat*, a poetic expression of love separation with an excursion in the background, into a travelogue in verse, replete with personal experience, social criticism and other content. This literary shift was accompanied by technological and economic changes: canals were opened up for trade and transport and the demand for labour loosened social constraints. By the late nineteenth century, pleasure had entered into the equation and the "father of Thai historiography," Prince Damrong, could write that the two aims of travel were pleasure and knowledge.[17] A traveller's desire was to escape old, depressing, familiar things and to visit, see, and have contact with an unfamiliar, exotic world. At the same time the desire to create what Thongchai has termed the geo-body of Siam resulted in a new provincial administration on a territorial basis. Rulers realised their lack of knowledge of Siam's interior and so they travelled inward to map out this territory. These travels were rendered into narratives producing knowledge of Siam's spatial "self." Travel, then, was a way of differentiating the Thai self from its others in Thongchai's estimation. Thongchai isn't explicit about the role of pilgrimage at this time, but he seems to equate it with older, "pre-modern" forms of travel and knowledge about space. These local and trans-local pilgrimages marked out a public space that was distinct from a national space. As religious authority became more centralised in Bangkok during the Fifth Reign, pilgrimage circuits opened up to accommodate performances of national identity. A cogent example of a state-founded pilgrimage site is Wat Phra Sri Mahathat, established in 1940 by the People's Party that overthrew the absolute monarchy.

25

---

15   Thongchai Winichakul, "The Others Within: Travel and Ethno-Spatial Differentiation of Siamese Subjects 1885–1910," in *Civility and Savagery: Social Identity in Tai States.* Andrew Turton, ed. (Surrey: Curzon, 2000), 41.

16   *Ibidem*, 42.

17   *Ibidem*, 43.

14 Prah Khan in Angkor Wat, Siem Reap. 2009

15 People worshiping at Huge Buddha in Wat Si Chum, Sukhothai. 1987

16 Myatheindan Pagoda, Mandalay. 1816

ORIGINALLY CALLED WAT PRACHATIPTAI [DEMOCRACY Wat], this new monastic
complex was not only built to house relics of the Buddha that had been brought
into Thailand from India, but to showcase the political ideals of nationalism and
equality that the People's Party promoted. Designed by architect Phra Phrahomphichit,
the temple was made of steel-reinforced concrete and eschewed much of the
royal symbolism of previous temples. Unlike royal temples, the *stupa* where the
Buddha relics were interred could be entereby commoners. The remains of the
leaders of the People's Party were later interred in the walls of the *stupa*, orbiting
around the Buddha relics. The *stupa* was not only a symbol of class equality but
also became a stage for performing rituals that were at once religious and political by
placing the bodies of living worshippers in relation to the remains of celestial as well
as profane beings.

II Pilgrimage and Violence

WHILE THE TENDENCY OF MOST religious scholars is to read the act of pilgrimage as
removed from or interrupted by violence, there is another relationship between
the moral communities formed around pilgrimage sites and an economy of
violence. Violence does not only refer to the coercive operations of the state or to
routine acts of violence directed against individuals, but also to crowd violence
that may erupt around pilgrimage sites. Tambiah, for instance, finds precedents
for the ritualised violence in various twentieth-century South and Southeast
Asian ethnic riots in religious beliefs, cultural practices and social customs.[18]
His account of the 1915 riots in Gampola, Ceylon, suggest that pilgrimage sites
can become contentious areas by asserting cultural authority over a territory,
as in the building of a new mosque by newly arrived "coast moors" from India.[19]
Tambiah describes how Sinhala Buddhist revivalism and nationalism came into
violent collision with evolving Islamic consciousness and identity, especially
when the economic activities of one newly arrived group ran counter to the
economic interests of another.[20]

---

18 Stanley J. Tambiah, *Leveling Crowds: Ethno-Nationalist Conflicts and Collective Violence in South Asia*
(Berkeley: University of California Press, 1996), 311.

19 *Ibidem*, 36.

20 *Ibidem*, 43.

17 *Siam by Clipper* [advertising poster].
Charles Baskerville, 1950

18 Temple of the Esmerald Buddha,
Bangkok. 1782–1784

While Tambiah's study is not centred on pilgrimage sites *per se*, he does point out that religious sites are intimately connected with the promotion of communal identities and violence. Tambiah asks whether the religious precedent of ritualised conduct in ethnic riots automatically legitimates that violence in ethical and moral terms. He suggests that religious violence was not random but had directed targets and that it merged with the realm of comedy and festivities, processions and Mardi Gras games.[21] To this I would add the act of pilgrimage.

I would like to suggest here that the same sites that are imbued with the sanctity of religious legitimacy and merit-making are also possible theatres for collective violence. My suggestion draws on the work of Walter Berkert, René Girard and Jonathan Z. Smith and their identification of collective violence as the heart of religious ritual. Girard suggests that violence is endemic to human society and there's no solution to this problem except for the answer religion gives in rituals of killing and their rationalisation as "sacrifice." All systems that structure human societies have been generated from sacrifice—language, kinship systems, taboos, codes of etiquette, patterns of exchange, rites and civil institutions.[22] Girard suggests that an act of mob violence stands at the beginning of human culture and that to bring the cycle of revenge violence to an end, a "final" killing is necessary. From within the group, one person is separated out as the victim. The victim must be vulnerable, unable to retaliate and without champions to continue the cycle of vengeful violence. There must also be unanimity within the group that the victim is the one at fault. Walter Berkert sees the Paleolithic hunt as an example of this Ur-act of collective violence.[23] Sacrifice, for Girard, Berkert, and Smith, is a rationalisation of this act of violence.

There is an intimate relationship between mob violence and religious morality that is related to Edward Palmer Thompson's idea of a "moral economy." Thompson argued that eighteenth-century food riots were a form of social protest. They were expressions of economic grievance that were based on the belief that the crowd was defending traditional rights or customs and were supported by the wider consensus of the community.[24] Economic grievances operated within a popular consensus about what was legitimate in marketing, milling, etc. This was grounded in a traditional view

---

21   *Ibidem*, 310.

22   Walter Berkert, René Girard & Jonathan Z. Smith, *Violent Origins. Walter Berkert, René Girard, Jonathan Z. Smith on Ritual Killing and Cultural Formation*. Robert G. Hammerton-Kelly, ed. (Stanford: Stanford University Press, 1987), 7.

23   *Ibidem*, 24.

24   *Ibidem* note 10.

19 Armed students hunddling during the riots of 1976 in Bangkok. 6th of October of 1976

20 Thai Police Standing Guard over student demostrators during the riots of 1976 in Bangkok. 6th of October of 1976

of the proper economic functions of different parties within the community. Such a "moral economy of the poor" was often at odds with eighteenth-century government policies. In the Siam of the early twentieth century Siam and the Thailand of the seventies, religious figures and Buddhist monks were active in shaping this moral economy with sometimes violent consequences. In the late nineteenth and early twentieth centuries, local pilgrimage sites in Siam became sites of violence during the *phu mi bun* or "men of merit" rebellions. During the same period, millennial movements in Siam suggest that these were largely local responses to sudden and radical shifts in conceptions of power and the implementation of provincial reforms by a newly centralised state.[25]

Buddhist teachings provide an explanation of the place of human beings in the natural cosmos and the social world. In the seventies, reformist monks of varying political allegiances exploited this role. One dramatic example is the conservative monk Kittiwuttho who suggested in the seventies that killing Communists did not contradict Buddhist doctrine. Kittiwuttho taught that social and economic inequality are determined by an individual's *kamma* and that equality in social status and wealth are as unattainable as equality in intelligence and physical ability.[26] Kittiwuttho's moral support of anti-Communist violence in the Thailand of the mid-seventies are described by several authors as influential in the violence that erupted in October, 1976. Up-country right-wing militias responded to media calls to assemble at public spaces in Bangkok and lynch left-wing university students in a public spectacle of bloodshed.[27]

Religious power, such as that exercised by Kittiwutho, operates through the discourse of felicity. As an instrument of power, felicity is a network that produces knowledge, pleasure and discourse and is not simply a negative, disciplining force.[28] In this way clerics could historically control what kings could not: the idea of what happens after death. The clergy added a transcendental gloss to mundane displays of power. The *wat*, the cathedral, the mosque and other religious landscape interventions were an important part of this discourse of felicity. These potent sites were physical evidence of what another world beyond this one might look like. As such, they were also instruments of power. Military control over large distances in pre-modern times may have required the use of

---

25 Charles F. Keyes, "Millennialism, Theravada Buddhism and Thai Society," *The Journal of Asian Studies,* vol. 36 n. 2 (Ann Arbor: The Association for Asian Studies, 1977): 285.

26 Peter A. Jackson, *Buddhism, Legitimation, and Conflict: the Political Functions of Urban Thai Buddhism* (Singapore: Institute of Southeast Asian Studies, 1989), 150.

27 *Ibidem*, 147–54; and Somboon Suksamran, *Buddhism and Politics in Thailand: A Study of Socio-political Change and Political Activism of the Thai Sangha* (Singapore: Institute of Southeast Asian Studies, 1982), 92–9.

28 Stephen Collins, *Nirvana and Other Buddhist Felicities: Utopias of the Pali Imaginaire* (Cambridge: Cambridge University Press, 1998), 19.

21

22

23

21 Buddha at Wat Mahathat, Sukhothai. 1345

22 Saint James on horseback [*Tumbo B: CF 33 f. 2v, detail*]. C. 1324

23 Archive of Galicia, City of Culture of Galicia. Manuel G. Vicente, 2010

local power holders but the centre doesn't only exert power through repressive means but through religious ideologies. The clergy, as holders of the ideological power of felicity, could co-operate with—but also challenge—those who had political, military and economic power. It could, for instance, justify extraction of tribute by ruling elites but it could also confront those elites with values, like asceticism, that they could not share.

Pilgrimage sites like the Cathedral of Santiago de Compostela and Wat Phra Sri Mahathat were important tools in making this discourse of felicity tangible to large numbers of people. They made the celestial present, but they were not simply symbols of power stranded within an empty landscape that could be easily apprehended by the uneducated masses. Sites that housed the relics of holy men were literal proof of their physical existence. They were brought to life by the bodies of the true believers who traversed the difficult routes of pilgrimage. Through acts of veneration and exchange, they made the violence of God present in the world.

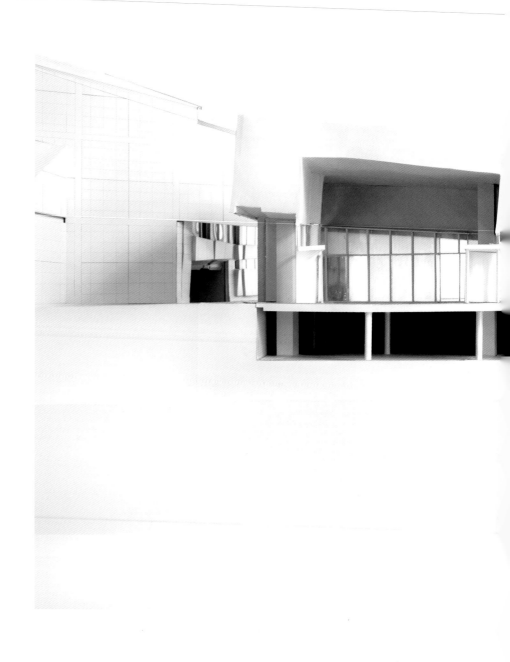

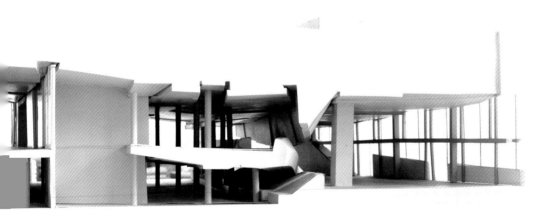

THE HISTORY
OF COMPOSTELA

—BOOK I. CXIV.

THE REBELLION
OF THE CONSPIRATORS
AGAINST THE BISHOP
AND THE QUEEN.
THE BURNING OF THE
CHURCH AND OTHER AFFAIRS

"De congressu conspiratorum in episcopum et in reginam et de incensa ecclesia et de ceteris.

Qualiter Arias Muniz apostatauit"

Historia Compostellana. Liber Primus, CXIV: Giraldus, *c.* 1120–1130

In the meantime the queen went to Lobeira and upon her return was received by the bishop of Iria; she then returned to Compostela, together with a great army of soldiers, for the queen had discussed with the bishop, her son and the illustrious people of Galicia how the slanderous comments made by the traitors to Compostela could be avenged and their pride dominated. She had assembled phalanxes of armed men, some of whom would enter with her and the bishop as arranged, while others would remain outside the city with her son. As they approached, the people of Compostela, well aware of their sin, realised that their reign was coming to a close, that they and their affairs were in a predicament and ended up regretting their deeds. What else? Some of sorrowful Judas's associates sought refuge in a church in Santiago, others in other churches, and others hid in their shelters. One of the ringleaders of the conspiracy pretended to take holy orders and so make sure his life was not in danger from the abbot or other monks in Saint Martin's church; wearing the habit he was able to escape from the queen's rage.

As regards those who remained in the Santiago church, the queen summoned the vicar and said, "Reverend Father, we would be grateful if your holiness would remove these despicable traitors from the church and give them the punishment they deserve; may the stench of this treason be banished from the church, this filthy dungheap cast out." To which the bishop replied, "My queen, it is unlawful for anybody to be forced out of the church after having sought refuge there, even if they be thieves, perjurers, traitors or criminals. Yet all their possessions outside the church should be handed over to plundering and taken by us." And the queen said, "Well, if they have the church as support and are safe there, why should they keep their weapons inside, if they feel secure and protected by the church? Why do they arm and protect themselves with other weapons? It is inadvisable for those who are safe in the church to seek any other protection. I order it to be banned and that either they lay down their arms and keep safe, as advisable, in the church or else if they remain armed the same number of our people or more should stay with them to ensure they do not dare act insanely."

The bishop and others who were present agreed with the queen's opinion and they were forbidden to take the weapons inside the church. When they learnt of the prohibition the traitors bellowed and after chasing through the church the messengers of the bishop and the queen who had told them to lay down their arms, they confronted them; those who reached the highest point of the church fled, the despicable traitors yelled war cries, the roar could be heard by all, the tempers of the traitors were discovered and what they had been trying to do for so long was made public. The entire city resounded, weapons were widespread and they rushed into fight. Fame, an evil faster than any other, spread that the soldiers of the bishop and the queen had attacked the people of Compostela. A few canons and citizens who had not been involved in the heinous madness intervened, attempting to appease the anger of their irate fellow citizens. But what could a few accomplish against a few thousands? The accomplices of the treason ran into combat; attracting acquaintances and friends they hoped to get rid of the bishop and the queen who had tried to get rid of them. After hearing the roar and din of the city and how Iscariotes's colleagues had incited the citizens against them, the bishop and the queen in the former's palaces were afraid, for they realised that the audacity of the traitors

was spreading and making the rebellion more violent, that the church in Santiago and the palaces were being besieged by groups of armed people and attacked even more fiercely. They were unaware of what decision to make against such a heinous madness. The church of the Apostle was captured after frequent assaults; stones, arrows and darts flew over the altar and irreverent fights were fought by the traitors. Is there anything that loathsome hands wouldn't tackle? The evil attackers set fire to the church of Santiago and did so on all sides, for much of the building was roofed with boards and straw. Oh, evilness! The church of the Apostle, so revered and so reputable, was burning and no honour was bestowed upon such a valued patron saint. Oh, sorrow! The flames of the church of the Apostle rose heavenwards and a horrific spectacle could be seen all around. All those present, Godfearing men and women, cried and moaned and cursed the authors of such an important crime. Oh! The weeping of the pilgrims who had travelled from different regions to revere the body of the Apostle!

3 &

Once they saw that the church was on fire and that the aforementioned crowd of accomplices were prepared to commit many evil deeds, instead of trusting the bishop's palaces the bishop and the queen sought refuge in the bell tower with his retinue. The citizens of Compostela went to the top of the church of the Apostle and made their way to the bishop's palace running, stealing and hurling. The clothes, gold and silver goblets and other things that had belonged to both the bishop and the queen were snatched, broken into pieces and taken as booty by the evil enemies: the citizens of Compostela went to the top of the church of Santiago, up to the tower in the bishop's palace and prepared to attack the belfry that had accommodated the bishop and his followers and knights, and the queen with hers. Some of these above the church, others in the towers and others on the ground attacked the belfry, throwing stones and launching arrows, threatening to kill the bishop the queen and their allies. The latter, however, who were in the bell tower with the bishop and the queen, defended themselves zealously, bearing in mind the place and the unequal number of people and returned the attacks. Here the clashes lasted longer. Eventually, when they saw that so few held out against such crowds and that the outcome of the fight was uncertain, the citizens of Compostela joined forces against the fire and by bringing their shields together over their heads they introduced fire through a window in the lower section of the tower,

after which they introduced combustible. Should I go on? The fire spread inside the tower and attacked those inside it.

4 &

When the bishop realised there would be no forgiveness either for him or for the queen, and that the crowd were wishing for his death, he spoke to her and to those inside and said, "Dear brothers, whether we are surrounded by a godless group of despicable people or in a desperate situation we have no refuge. Our only refuge and comfort is God, the refuge of the oppressed, the comfort of the sorrowful: let's place our hope and trust in God, who can rescue us from the hands of the heathen and free us of such great danger. For He rescued Daniel from the lake of the lions, He rescued the three boys, Sidrac, Misac and Abdenago from the furnace of burning fire. Let's convert God sincerely and He will convert us. For he said, *Convert Me and I will convert you.* Let us repent of our offences and sins. Let us confess each other's sins and pray for one another that we are saved; let us invoke God's mercy for him to pardon our sins and deigned to grant us his mercy. He who lives for ever and ever." Upon hearing these words the queen and all those present burst into tears and confessed to the bishop.

f. 41

5

Then the queen, turning to the bishop, said, "Father, come out of the fire so that I can come out with you. For you would be pardoned like their patron saint, their bishop and their lord." Then the bishop said, "This is not good advice. For they consider themselves our enemies and wish specifically for our death." From outside they cried, "Let the queen come out, if she desires; she alone has our permission to come out and the power to live, may the others perish by the sword and by fire." Hearing that, as inside the fire was reviving and even the bishop urged her to leave, and once the safety of the attackers had been guaranteed the queen left the tower. When the mob saw her come out they leapt on her and threw her into a quagmire, seizing her like wolves and tearing her clothes; naked from the chest down, in front of everyone she remained shamefully on the ground for a long time. There were also many who wanted to stone her to death, among them an old lady from Compostela who caused her serious injury by hurling a stone at her cheek.

6

In the meantime, while the bishop was praying inside and the flames were rising, the abbot of Saint Martin's came to see him and gave him a crucifix. After welcoming him

the bishop went into confession and then left the tower as if ready to face the ordeal. Leaving his cloak and taking an unworthy cape from someone, how impressive!, holding the crucifix in front of his face he crossed the line of combat, the ranks of the fiercest enemies, making his way through the weapons of the wicked traitors, over three thousand of them, and was only recognised by one. Upon reaching the spot where the queen lay in the mud, trampled on by the enemy mobs, and seeing her so shamefully naked and abandoned he felt so aggrieved that he left and passed through the church of Santiago to reach Saint Mary's church alongside the canon Miguel González, who then accompanied him in his adversities. Then he received the body and blood of the Lord and was able to rest more assuredly.

7

Meanwhile, a few canons who knew that he had left arrived to make enquiries, and asked whether the bishop had escaped the danger of the fire and the armed people or whether he had remained in the tower, prepared to die. But the bishop, aware of their treachery, asked Miguel and the others who were protecting him beside the altar to get them away from there. However, as they couldn't remove them unless they had been told that the bishop had escaped and was safe, after swearing that they would tell nobody of his salvation, they were informed of what had taken place and how, and they left. Finally the queen, her hair dishevelled, her body naked and covered in mud, got away and arrived at the same church in which the bishop had been hiding, despite having no knowledge of him.

8 ❦

Those who had remained in the tower, once they saw how the flames had reached the full height of the building, jumped off the top and got away, while others threw themselves amidst the lines of armed people. Pedro, prior of the church of Santiago (whom we have mentioned earlier), the bishop's nephew, made his way through the enemy lines and skilfully managed to escape, as did many others. Gundesindo Gelmírez, the bishop's brother, was pierced by lances and spears as he made his way through. Rodrigo Oduáriz, the bishop's majordomo, Ramiro, his chef, and Diego "The Cross-eyed," the vicar of the city were also killed in the same spot, while others managed to escape, wounded, robbed and half dead.

The bishop ordered a messenger to inform the queen, who was hiding in Saint Mary's church, that he had escaped from the fire and was hiding in the same church. When she learnt the news while weeping for her own dishonour and heartache she was pleased, although she concealed the motive of her joy in fear that the persecutors would discover the fact.

9 ❦

After that, the inhabitants of Compostela appeared before the queen at Saint Mary's and showing signs of joy for her salvation they guarded her and filled the church with weapons to defend her. Partly fearing for herself and partly for their learning of the bishop's presence, the queen spoke thus to their troops: "Go, you evil people, go, you wicked people, go, you reprobates, to the tower in which your bishop is dying by the sword and by fire. Wrench him from the danger as soon as possible to avoid being considered by posterity as an example of so much wickedness and sacrilege. Go, I say, rebels and unbelievers, and prevent such a horrific crime from being committed." She said this to get them away and make sure they didn't make any assumptions about the bishop. Hearing these shouts, the mobs that had arrived moved away towards the tower. They repelled those who were still attacking it by pouring combustible on to the fire, and all together shouted for water, which they tipped inside, extinguishing the fire as far as they could and endeavouring to release the bishop. Some of the canons, the widows, the orphans, the poor and a number of citizens wept for him, for the fire had reached such a height that if the bishop had still been in the tower by then he would have turned into ashes. The tower, the beams and the boards were burnt, and the bronze bells that weighed one thousand five hundred pounds were also burnt and fell to the ground.

10 &

Once the queen had repelled the people's attack on Saint Mary's church by means of the strategy we have described, she herself fled to Saint Martin's church, where she would be safer. After furtively leaving Saint Mary's to escape the crowds and the attack of the people, in the company of aforesaid Miguel and of two Frenchmen the bishop climbed walls and roofs and got in the window of a house belonging to a said Maurino. Covered by pieces of cloth and other such objects, the bishop and his companions hid in a corner of the house until four armed men who were looking for him on behalf of the traitors asked, "Who's hiding there? What's going on? Have you seen the man we're looking for, the bishop?" Hearing these words the

bishop and Miguel hid amidst a stack of cloths and dresses. If they hadn't done so they would have been killed there and then. When the armed men arrived the two Frenchmen got up saying they were resting there, tired of their efforts during the uproar and skirmishes. The mistress of the house who knew the bishop was hiding there arrived on the scene and reprimanded the men, calling them invaders. After accusing them of spying on her home she forced them to leave. The two Frenchmen left with them, in order to ensure protection of the bishop. Such was the ineffable mercy of almighty God, who freed the bishop from danger seizing him from the very hands of these wickedest of men!

Once they had been removed, Gonzalo, the lady's soninlaw, appeared, and said, "Come out, father and lord, escape as quickly as you can, hide away, for this loathsome group of traitors, stained by the blood of others and still thirsty for yours, is looking everywhere for you. I've seen them make their way here with swords and sticks. Get away swiftly and make no more stops. God is able to free you from the hands of the heathen, from the fauces of those who hope to devour you." Upon hearing these words the bishop got up and after Gonzalo himself had broken the partition wall of the house next door, and then another, and then a third, he reached

Froilán Rudesíndez's house which stood at the heart of the city. The mistress of the house began to shout that some assailants had entered her home and were looting it. Miguel replied that an acquaintance and a friend of her husband's, Froilán Menéndez, major-domo to the queen, had escaped the internal insurrection and the revolts and skirmishes and had sought refuge in that house. Shortly afterwards Froilán Rudesíndez, the master of the house, arrived; as soon as he learnt the bishop was there he ran towards him sobbing, "Thank God, dearest father, who has freed you from such great danger and has led you here, safe and sound. Yet we must fear an enemy attack and beware in case as they move from one place to another they should find and kill you, for they are prepared for committing all sorts of crimes. So, come with me." And he led him and Miguel to a dark pantry in the cellar and for a long time they stood there weeping.

11 𝄞

In the meantime, the aforementioned Frenchmen prepared four fast horses for the bishop, so that at dusk, moving to the other part of the neighbourhood and from there through the fields of Saint Martin's he, Miguel and the others could mount them and gallop away. But it all turned out very differently, for after making these preparations P., abbot of Saint Pelayo's, appeared with one of his monks, Pelayo Díaz and P., prior of the canons and the bishop's nephew, saying "We were sent to you by the clergy and the people of the city. They are sorry for having acted badly towards you; they love you as their lord and bishop and must give you satisfaction. Between five hundred and a thousand men are waiting for you in the cloister of Saint Pelayo's, clergymen and laymen alike, prepared to swear their love and loyalty to you and seek your presence. So, leave this nook behind and come and be reconciled with them. If you believe us, they've never been as subjugated as they are today." All this had been plotted by the traitors so that, deceiving the messengers, they could at least find the bishop and then kill him. As the messengers had forced the bishop to come out and had reprimanded him, in view of the fact that he was aware of the deception and of the traitors' intentions, he said, "Go and see the five hundred or one thousand men you speak of and tell them I'm safe and sound; don't tell any of them where I am. If, as you assure, a hundred of them should swear in the names of all the others, I will stand before them tomorrow." Oh, what wisdom the man showed, the grace of God realised in advance what those wicked men had plotted and how! The messengers then left, but found no one to bear out their promise. They eventually discovered the contrivance of the fraud and betrayal: if the bishop had believed them, following their reckless advice, he would have fallen into the hands of his enemies and would perhaps have been killed by them. The aforesaid prior, having learnt of the fraud and betrayal, amazed and frightened, remained safely inside the church.

12 &

Accompanied by the monk we have spoken of, the abbot went back to the bishop and told him of the fraud and the traitors' lies, schemes that the bishop had wisely sensed. Then, at dusk, the abbot and the monk secretly took the bishop and Miguel to his church, i.e., Saint Pelayo's, and led him to the treasury behind the backs of the other monks, with the exception of the treasurer. After that the abbot spoke to the bishop and said, "Be reassured, father, and be strong, have some food so you may recover," for the bishop still hadn't eaten anything. To which the bishop replied, "It's not advisable for me to break my fast if I am to die tomorrow when my enemies cut my throat. Only God's mercy and compassion, which rescued me today from such great dangers, will be able to do so again tomorrow, if He so wishes." However, condescending to the abbot's pleads, he took a little bread and wine and rested. Clearer than light is the fact that that night the bishop didn't succumb to sleep but sought comfort in psalms and prayers, and when the monks rose for Matins he himself rose and through the window in the treasury he listened to the monks' morning service.

13 &

Finally, at dawn the next day, Sunday, all the accomplices in the betrayal gathered at the canonry, attracting the clergy and the people partly with threats and partly with gifts. They were sure that their evil conspiracy had borne fruit and that like kings they governed over all. They were presided over by a godless and extremely wicked man who had dwelt in Compostela throughout the conspiracy. As ringleader of the conspirators he had incited many of the accomplices, and with all his heart hoped to gain control of the church of Santiago, for by then the subordinates had divided up among themselves the whole domain of Santiago and had established how much of it would go to each individual. So, after gathering at the canonry, the aforementioned heathen exhorted them to strengthen their fraternity and remain united, to fortify their city with a wall and a fence and expel their enemies, should there still be any among them. They resolved to make it up with the queen, satisfying her after the dishonour and the insults she had suffered the day before and establishing a firm peace alliance. They sent those who discussed such issues with her to see the queen, who was still hiding from them in Saint Martin's church, and they asked her about the bishop, whether he had managed to escape or was still in hiding, and what were the feelings he aroused among the clergy and the people. One of these, whom the bishop loved and trusted for he had educated him, stood up and in front of them all stated the following, "Brothers, he who has been up until now our lord and bishop is no longer worthy of ruling over us or of being our bishop, for he reduced the dignity of your church and grievously oppressed you with the yoke of his dominion. Furthermore, to ensure that none of you declare him your lord or bishop I confess before God and Santiago and before you that from this moment on he will cease to be my lord. I am ready to prove that he deserved what has happened to him and that he must give up all his dominions." The bishop had educated this dreadful man in his palace since childhood and had honoured him at the church of Santiago; as an adult, the bishop had sent him to France to learn grammar, after having given him quite a lot of money, and upon his return he had treated him on very familiar and close terms, almost making him the lord of his house and bestowing paternal affection on him.

He had also given him large sums of money, receiving practically no gifts from him in exchange, and a good prebend—Arnois, half of Serantes, Cée, half of Santa Cristina de Noya and much more. Oh, perfidious Galician loyalty! The bishop had educated this dreadful man with a father's pride; he had loved him, showered him with honours and benefits while he, forgetting everything and repaying good for evil, wished for the destruction and death of the bishop. After he had concluded the aforesaid harangue, a part of the clergy and of the people, imbued with the same poison, praised his words and judged that that was how things should be. Those who had played no part in the betrayal or conspired against the bishop or the queen and hated such decisions, despite finding such wickedness disagreeable and having a different opinion of the bishop and the others, dared not contradict them or even open their mouths, for if they should have dared say or do anything against their will among so many accomplices of Judas's their houses would immediately have been destroyed, their assets taken as booty and perhaps they themselves buried under a mountain of stones. In the words of Solomon, there is "*A time to keep silence and a time to speak.*"

[…]

f. 47

The Future is Here

Santiago de Compostela's Call to the World

Ismail Serageldin

The city atop the hill: A spectacular mix of order and controlled chaotic geometries, a marvel of form that dictates function and speaks with subtlety to the past, while rushing headlong into the future. This project is particularly well-suited to its task at this junction between two eras. From a moment when order ruled to one where complexity and chaos are the norm. It is a moment when human civilisation teeters on the brink of a new world system and is witnessing a revolution that affects as to the structure and meaning of knowledge, as to how we will most likely be interacting with knowledge, whether we are academics or researchers or simply the descendants of those who used to go to public libraries and ask the librarian for assistance with a good book to read or a reference source for the paper they are preparing for college: the production and dissemination of knowledge, its storage and retrieval, its understanding and manipulation, its interpretation and reinterpretation, its integration and reinvention, all necessary parts of a functional legacy and a dynamic cultural scene, will be different. If the diagnosis is correct, then we should be thinking from now as to how to design the infrastructure of the supporting structures of knowledge and culture that are archives, libraries and museums.

1 *The Tower of Babel.* Pieter Bruegel "The Elder," 1563

2 Library of Galicia, City of Culture of Galicia. Manuel G. Vicente, 2010

I A Visionary Enterprise

THE CITY ATOP THE HILL. The city as it has never been before, except in our wildest
dreams and our greatest longings … A spectacular mix of order and controlled chaotic
geometries, that only a true master of the stature of Peter Eisenman could achieve.
A marvel of form that dictates function and speaks with subtlety to the past, while
rushing headlong into the future, declaring boldly: "I am the future."

THE UNIQUE ARCHITECTURE IS SKILFULLY geometric and at the same time provides
unusual spaces that challenge the mind and the eye. The six buildings are spatially
interconnected by streets and plazas but share a common foundation, a common
infrastructure, that includes enormous state-of-the-art technology. Together the
buildings and the open spaces that link them are a worthy creation for inspiration,
reflection, debate and actions oriented towards Galicia's future. The quality of
the products that will be displayed there, and those which will be born out of this
reflection and inspiration will guarantee the internationalisation of Galicia's role as
Santiago de Compostela becomes synonymous with the challenge of the new, and
the city and the region remain synonymous with the memory of the past and the
custodianship of its heritage.

BEING ROOTED IN THE PAST does not mean that we are prisoners of its legacy.
Respect, yes, but no slavish copying of forms that are no longer needed or practices
that are now obsolete and quaint at best. That does not mean that we forget the
past, for we would be like amnesiacs lacking an important part of our identity. It does
not mean that we should not protect the heritage of the past, for these magnificent
monuments are witnesses of past grandeur or exemplars of special periods of our
history, and they shall forever remain the touchstones of our memory and the
wellsprings for our imagination. But it does mean that we must use this imagination
to design the contemporary and the new. We must create the heritage of tomorrow
through our actions of today.

THIS DUAL TASK OF HOSTING services and activities devoted to the preservation of
heritage and memory while at the same time providing the means and the space,
physically and metaphorically, for the study, research, experimentation and
production of the new, is difficult to achieve. However, I believe that this design
and the organisations housed in the buildings will manage it. And I believe that the
results will be seen in the quality of the output in terms of literature, music, drama,
dance, film, the visual arts, audiovisual creation and communication. For all these
fields will benefit from the link to the best of the past, just as they will benefit from the
new technologies that will emerge out of the new knowledge revolution.

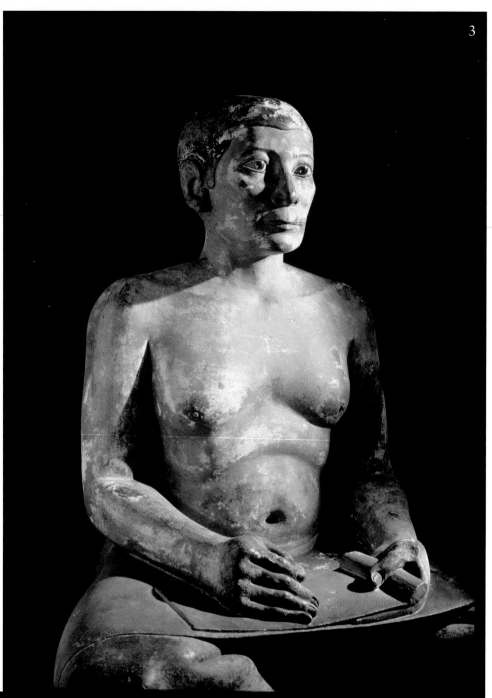

3

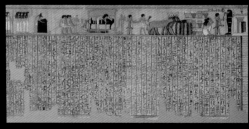

4

3 *The Seated Scribe.*
C. 2620– 2500 BC

4 Papyrus of Nebqed [*Book of Dead*: chap. 125, detail].
C. 664–332 BC

THIS PROJECT IS PARTICULARLY WELL suited to its task at this intersection between two eras, between a moment when order ruled and one where complexity and chaos (in the scientific sense of the term) are the norm. This is a moment when human civilisation is teetering on the brink of a new world system … for we are witnessing a revolution in the structure and meaning of knowledge that is more profound than anything humanity has known since the invention of writing! Writing, not printing. For the former allowed the accumulation and transmission of knowledge across space and time and enabled primitive agglomerations to become thriving civilisations. Printing merely spread the benefits of reading by multiplying the number of copies of manuscripts that could be produced accurately and inexpensively. That is no mean feat in itself, but it is far less significant than the invention of writing.

So AM I EXAGGERATING WHEN I compare the current revolution to the invention of writing? I think not, and I believe that the evidence that I shall assemble will satisfy the reader that this is indeed the case.

GREAT ARTISTS CAN SOMEHOW SENSE the *Zeitgeist*, and even contribute to creating it, as Peter Eisenman did in this pioneering project. He sensed that the future is more than a mere extension of the past. He sensed that we need roots and links to our past, but that we need to be the artisans of the new and revel in the exaltation and freedom of innovation. Freedom is artfully expressed interacting effortlessly with the boundaries of subtle geometries.

EISENMAN'S MASTERPIECE IS POISED BETWEEN the past and the future, asserting its presence and yet melding with its environment. It is a *tour de force* that few would be able to contemplate, much less ably deliver. Galicia has its masterpiece. Just as Bilbao was redefined by the Frank O. Gehry's museum, I feel certain that despite Galicia's magnificent past it will be defined for decades to come by Eisenman's creation. For Galicia, exceptionally well-rooted in the past of Hispanic culture, is eager to help establish her future in a rapidly changing world. The City of Culture of Galicia at Santiago de Compostela is the capstone of a long campaign to redefine the city and the launching pad for a new era of cultural institutions serving a new world order defined by the new knowledge revolution.

ROOTED IN THE RICH TRADITION of the past, Santiago de Compostela is an emblem of European cultural tradition, a historic city that was declared a World Heritage Site by UNESCO in 1985. The City of Culture of Galicia has taken the essence of its traditional past and translated it into an enchanting futuristic vision on the top of mount Gaiás. It speaks to the present and prefigures the future, as it opens to host the best cultural expressions of Galicia, Spain, Europe, Latin America and the world at large. The ecumenicalism and pluralism of this new inclusive and sophisticated "city"

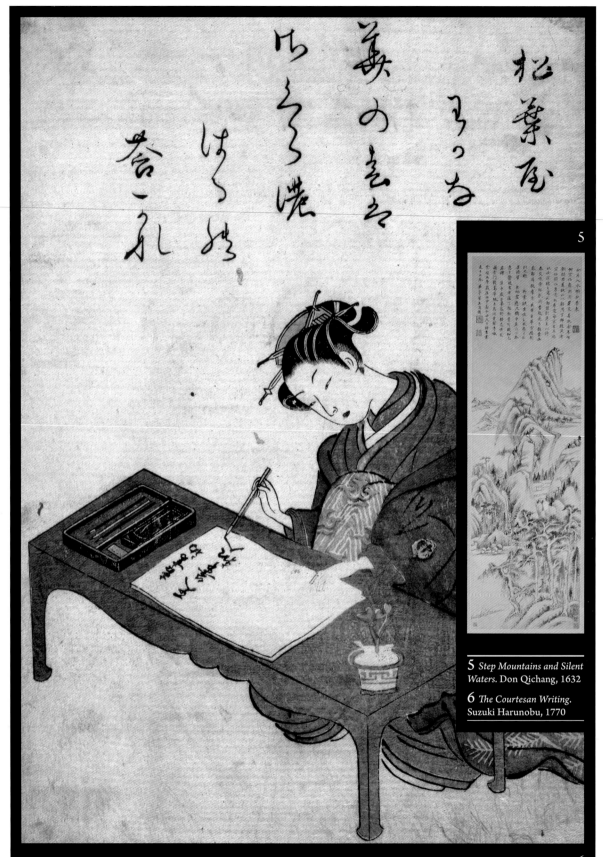

松葉屋 みつる 美の志ら はう港 はちめ 荅一礼

5 *Step Mountains and Silent Waters.* Don Qichang, 1632

6 *The Courtesan Writing.* Suzuki Harunobu, 1770

shall be at the forefront when it comes to meeting the challenges of the information and knowledge society. How? Well, let us first try and discover a bit more about where the new knowledge revolution is taking us, and the world.

II The Seven Pillars of the New Knowledge Revolution

We all agree that we are rapidly moving towards a society based on knowledge and an economy based on technology, a transformation overlaid by the well-documented aspects of globalisation. I am referring to the structure and the presentation of knowledge and to how we are likely to interact with it, whether we are academics or researchers or simply the descendants of those who used to visit public libraries and ask for assistance to find a good book to read or a reference source for a college paper. This is what I call the "new knowledge revolution," a subject I have treated elsewhere at length and in more technical detail[1] and that can be diagnosed by seven key characteristics I call "pillars," and which I shall briefly describe:

   i Parsing, Life and Organisation
  ii Image and Text
 iii Human Beings and Machines
 iv Complexity and Chaos
  v Computation and Research
 vi Convergence and Transformation
vii Pluridisciplinary Approaches and Policies

A word about each of these seven pillars is pertinent here.

First. Parsing, Life and Organisation

Since the beginning of time, whether we were writing on scrolls or on codices, whether the codices were printed or manuscripts, the accumulation of knowledge was based on parsed structures, with units standing side by side like bricks in the wall of an emerging structure. It was the juxtaposition of these individual parsed works that created the accumulation of knowledge; the rising edifice built piece by piece, brick by brick or stone by stone.

---

1 See my rather lengthy monograph *The Seven Pillars of the Knowledge Revolution* (Alexandria: Bibliotheca Alexandrina, 2010).

7 The printer's workshop
[*The Book of Trades*: p. 19, detail]. Jost Amman, 1568

MOREOVER, EACH PIECE WAS "DEAD." In other words, once published, it stayed as it was until a second edition appeared. If two of us had copies of the same book, we could both open it on, say, page 157 and find exactly the same thing in our respective copies. It made no difference whether we did it immediately after the book appeared or decades later.

THE INTERNET CHANGED ALL THAT.

THE WEB PAGE BECAME THE unit of parsing. Instead of the classical sequence of presentation, we now think in terms of a home page and then hypertext links to other related documents. We can expect more fluidity in the merging of images, both stills and videos, and in the transitions from one reference link to another. Search engines complement the World Wide Web as on-line material (unlike traditionally published material) becomes alive. If two people look up the same website, at the same location, with a few hours' difference it will probably have changed, since the material is constantly updated.

FURTHERMORE, AS WE MOVE BEYOND the current structures of the web towards those of the semantic web, where we can search for relationships and concepts instead of just objects, the structure of organisation and presentation of knowledge will become one large interconnected vibrant living tissue of concepts, ideas and facts that will grow exponentially and will require new modes of thinking to interact with it, modes of thinking that will be automatically spawn and therefore scholarship will be no longer be parsed like bricks in a wall, but will resemble a smooth flowing river.

IF WE WERE TO TAKE into account the new phenomena of social linkages brought about by the Internet and the World Wide Web we would be able to visualise what some specialists have called the "meta-web," characterised by high knowledge connectivity and high social connectivity. Does the meta-web prefigure the connectivity of intelligence?

Second. Image and Text

THROUGHOUT HISTORY, WRITTEN TEXT HAS been the primary means for the transmission of information. Images were difficult to produce and to reproduce. This has now changed. Thanks to the digital revolution everybody is able to record still and video images, and computer-generated graphics are easily affordable.

THE HUMAN BRAIN CAN PROCESS visual information extremely quickly, and enormous detail can be captured and processed in a fraction of a second. So some new features of the current knowledge revolution seem imminent. One is a far greater reliance on images—in addition to text—in the communication of information and knowledge, which will entail new storage and retrieval devices as we move from text-dependent books and journals to digital still and video image presentations, three-dimensional

8 *Study of the Head of Saint Anne.* Leonardo da Vinci, *c.* 1510

9 *Metropolis* [advertising poster]. Werner Graul, 1926

virtual reality and holographic presentations. Interactivity will also become a feature of this new image-based virtual reality world. Again, what does this entail in terms of presentation, search and retrieval functions and the interaction between researchers and material in the future?

THE EFFECTIVE DESCRIPTION IN META-DATA, storage, the searchable and retrievable nature of this vast and still growing world of fixed and interactive still and moving images? We shall cease to look up images through key words entered into text databases or meta-data catalogues—computers will do this for us.

Third. Human Beings and Machines

WITH THE EXCEPTION OF PURE mathematics and of some aspects of Philosophy, it will no longer be possible for individuals to search for, find, retrieve and then manipulate knowledge in any field, much less add to it and make their contribution public without the intermediation of machines. Even in literary criticism and the social sciences, the stock of available material can no longer be searched manually.

THIS IS NEITHER GOOD NOR bad, it's just a fact.

NOW, AFTER IBM's SPECIAL CHESS playing programme "Big Blue" defeated world chess champion Gary Kasparov in 1997 we could indeed ask ourselves, as some visionaries are doing, whether "consciousness" and "intelligence" are qualities that emanate from very complex systems. According to some authors, in all likelihood within the first half of the twenty-first century we shall bear witness to all this—as soon as machines cross the thresholds of complexity and power, and processing power reaches a certain level, followed by software advances a decade or so later.

AND YET, WHATEVER THE MERITS of that particular debate and its ramifications may be, it is obvious that changes are already noticeable in the domain of libraries and the Internet, as exemplified by the new World Digital Library, a system which allows video, image text, commentary and maps to be linked together in one seamless whole. Searchable through many different approaches (time, geography, theme, cluster, or even a single word), it enables us to browse the material and find what we are looking for from among the digitised material on offer from around the world.

Fourth. Complexity and Chaos

WE LIVE IN A REMARKABLY complex world, a globalised world in which socioeconomic transactions are exceedingly intricate and the "click" of a mouse and the flight of an electron can send billions of dollars around the planet at the speed of light. The web of interconnected transactions is enormous, and the ripple effects of any single set of actions and its interaction with other effects are extremely difficult to predict.

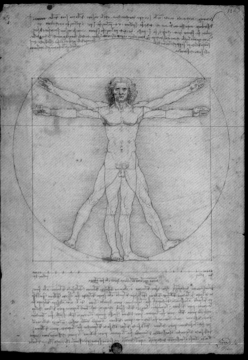

10 *Vitruvian Man*. Leonardo da Vinci, 1492

11 Brigitte Helm as the Robot Maria in *Metropolis*. Fritz Lang, 1926

12 Chess player Garry Kasparov plays against IBM's supercomputer "Deep Blue." 5th of May of 1997

NOT ONLY HAVE OUR CITIES become much larger but also much more complex, and ecosystems are delicate and, like biological systems, intrinsically intricate.

REALITY IS COMPLEX AND CHAOTIC, and complex systems have non-linear feedback loops that result in systems and subsystems which are highly difficult to anticipate. Many of our models, based on the simple mathematics and analogies drawn from Physics, are proving inadequate.

Fifth. Computation and Research

BROADLY SPEAKING, COMPUTING TO DATE has been regarded as the extension of a large calculating machine that is capable of making simple calculations at incredible speeds. Computer scientists and engineers were seen as implementers who made the lives of creators and researchers less tedious. Wonderful tools, no doubt, but tools all the same. Today, the concepts and the techniques of computing have become central to the new research paradigm. Computational science concepts, tools and theorems are being woven into the very fabric of science and scientific practice.

SUFFICE IT TO CONSIDER DATA management. Data, when organised, becomes information and information, when explained, becomes knowledge. In turn and coupled with reflection, insight and experience, knowledge may lead to wisdom, but that is another story.

BEYOND THEIR SCALE AND MAGNITUDE, however, we are looking for connections between sets of data, and these connections pose particular problems that entail qualitatively different issues. Most of the work carried out on such problems belongs to the field of computer science.

Sixth. Convergence and Transformation

DOMAINS ARE GRADUALLY CONVERGING. In simple terms, once upon a time we had Chemistry and Biology as distinct and separate enterprises; now we have Biochemistry. Such moments of convergence, generating new sciences and insights, have proved to be some of the most fecund moments in the evolution of our knowledge and the development of our technologies. Today we are witnessing the convergence of three hitherto separate fields with the birth of "BINT:" Bio/Info/Nano Technology.

AT THE SAME TIME, we need to develop what the National Science Foundation (NSF), calls transformative research, i.e., research capable of changing the paradigm in certain fields and domains, like Synthetic Biology and Femtochemistry. This research is extremely valuable, and has given rise to entirely new fields such as Genomics, Proteomics and Metabolomics thanks to the discovery of the structure and mechanism of DNA.

14

THE QUESTION WE ARE FACING now is whether such developments will remain serendipitous or whether our research paradigm will systematically force the development of such converging domains and transformative insights. I believe we are poised to move in the second direction.

Seventh. Pluridisciplinary Approaches and Policies

THERE IS REAL VALUE IN crossing disciplines. Increasingly, both in the academic world and when it comes to tackling real-life problems, we note that the old "silos" of disciplines are counterproductive. Much of the most interesting work is being carried out in between disciplines, where these intersect or at their interstices.

WE ARE BECOMING INCREASINGLY AWARE of the fact that real-life problems such as poverty, gender or the environment are all multidimensional and complex and require a special way of organising their different disciplinary inputs. Just as we consider diversity enriching, so is the sharing of knowledge across disciplines.

AS A RESULT OF THE nature of the challenge, its scale and complexity, many people require interactional expertise in order to improve their efficiency working across multiple disciplines as well as within the new interdisciplinary area.

III Epilogue—Implications of the Knowledge Revolution

General Implications

IT IS CLEAR FROM THE preceding discussion that we are entering a new age in which the production and dissemination of knowledge, its storage and retrieval, its understanding and manipulation, its interpretation and reinterpretation, its integration and reinvention—all of which are necessary parts of a functional cultural legacy and a dynamic cultural scene—will have changed.

IF OUR DIAGNOSIS IS CORRECT, then we should be considering how to design the infrastructure of knowledge in our societies, taking into account the "seven pillars of the new knowledge revolution," as I have chosen to call them, and their implications. By infrastructure I mean the education system from pre-school to post-graduate studies, the research institutions in universities, independent laboratories and the private sector, and the supporting structures of knowledge and culture such as libraries, archives and museums.

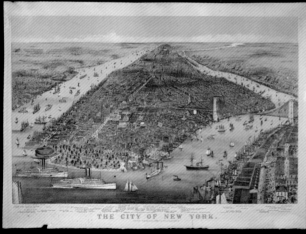

15 Map of Alexandria [*Civitates Orbis Terrarum*, George Braun & Frans Hogenberg: vol. II n. 56]. Joris Hoefnagel, *c.* 1573

16 *The City of New York*. Charles Parsons, 1876

17 *Empirical Construction, Istambul*. Julie Mehretu, 2003

Implications for Libraries and Museums

THE IMPLICATIONS FOR LIBRARIES AND museums are profound. All storage and retrieval functions are prone to technical and physical obsolescence. Despite their enormous convenience and their ability to expand our mental and physical reach in many innovative ways, new digital technologies are highly susceptible of swiftly becoming obsolete.

The Future of Libraries

THE EXPERIENCE OF THE WORLD Digital Library (WDL) provides a glimpse of what the future may hold for libraries. One of the questions it raises is that of their purpose now that all material can be presented in virtual formats and brought to us wherever we happen to be, whether at home or at the office. The new institutions of the third millennium will fulfil at least five special functions.

i   They will continue to keep originals. Manuscripts and first editions will continue to fascinate us as objects of intrinsic value and worth, over and above their contents. Being able to consult them will confer on the visitor special joys and possibly new insights.

ii Libraries will become meeting places for the like-minded and for people interested in specific subjects. Treasured meeting places, evoking the past and surrounded by the treasures of our heritage, they will be inspiring venues for literati and the general public alike.

iii For institutional and monetary reasons, certain material will continue to be beyond the reach of most people and only obtainable *in situ* and for a nominal fee at libraries. Furthermore, libraries will have integrated infrastructures for researchers, artists and critics which will make a full range of materials and facilities available in one and the same place equipped with excellent services.

iv Libraries will be ideal bridges between the general public, particularly researchers, and the national and international archiving system. The sheer scale of the enterprise will pose particular problems that only libraries and archiving institutions will be able to address.

v   Libraries will continue to develop specific programmes involving children, teenagers, schools and parents in the wonderful venture of socialisation and learning that will exist as long as societies continue to exist. Such a venture may change in content as the world around us evolves, especially in the radical manner that I have described, but it will continue nonetheless. The transition from childhood to adulthood entails much more than a transfer of skills, it involves the learning of who we are and where we belong. Culture expresses itself at every turn and cultural institutions will therefore still be a part of the future we are looking to, as much as they have been part of our past.

18 *Labyrinth City Project.* Leon Krier, 1971

19 *Metropolis* [advertising poster]. Heinz Schulz-Neudamm, 1926

20 Volumetric scheme from City of Culture of Galicia's buildings tridimensional study. Eisenman Architects, 2010

The Future of Museums

Museums will have to become much more than storage places for rare originals and general imparters of knowledge. Yes, we will always experience that unique joy, that special feeling of awe in the presence of the actual original piece of art or the rare object recognised as a "museum piece," and experts may well discover additional and possibly profound insights that can be gained only by the examination of original works. But museums are not only for connoisseurs; they have to cater to the needs and wants of the general public. They must be aware of the fact that the World Wide Web will provide excellent materials in very lifelike 3-D animations, and will provide access to many sources of information. Thus the adisplays of tomorrow will become more like curated exhibitions, perpetually changing as the institution tries to reach the public in myriad ways. The skill of curators will be apparent in the quality of the shows they organise. So rather than standardised fare, we can expect the museums of tomorrow to present displays in perpetual change, that will make full use of available technologies but will be enhanced by an added "oomph" as a result of their size, spatial excellence, attractive surroundings and the exciting manner in which the buildings themselves provide a sense of place.

Envoi

Back to the architectural project. The seven pillars of the knowledge revolution, the definers of the new culture of the twenty-first century, find their architectural echo in the six buildings that together define much of the activity. Each one is as important as each of the six pillars that define the meaning of knowledge today. The seventh pillar, the pluridisciplinary approaches that derive from the integrative understanding that emerges once all the pieces have been brought together, is also echoed in Galicia's remarkable City of Culture on the hill. The seventh pillar of Eisenman's creation is the whole. Indeed, in this project the whole is much more than the sum of the parts. The project must be regarded as an integrated whole, and that is precisely the seventh pillar. Just as knowing implies having recourse to all the components of knowledge, including pluridisciplinary approaches, in order to grasp its multifaceted reality, seeing how the five avenues connect the six buildings is essential to understanding how they form an organic whole erected on the mountain, becoming a part of it rather than being just built on its top, embedded in it and yet distinct from it.

Have we even begun to plumb the depth of the design and its implications? I think not. Only the actual use that the foundations make of it will bring the superb buildings to life and make the space all it can inherently become. With hindsight, we shall learn the measure of that success. At present, we can only raise questions and express hopes.

21 *Scholars studying in Library of Alexandria.* 1901

22 Schoolchildren in the Egyptian section of The British Museum, London. C. 1960

23 The new Reading Room at The British Museum, London [*The Illustrated London News*]. 1857

24 Students in the reading room of the Library of Congress, Washington DC. Frances Benjamin Johnston, 1899

CAN WE EVEN CLAIM TO have properly sketched out the full range of implications that the seven pillars of the new knowledge revolution will force upon us? Do we know how the technologies that lie ahead of us will affect our ability to summon the spirit of the past and conjure inspiring images to help us create a new future? Who can tell?

IT IS TRUE THAT THERE are no complete or even fully satisfying answers to many questions implicit in the discussions above. However, in this modern age, to quote Boorstin, we are "questers" who realise that knowledge and cultural expression are a journey and not a destination, and that the fruitfulness of the questions is more important than the finality of the answers.

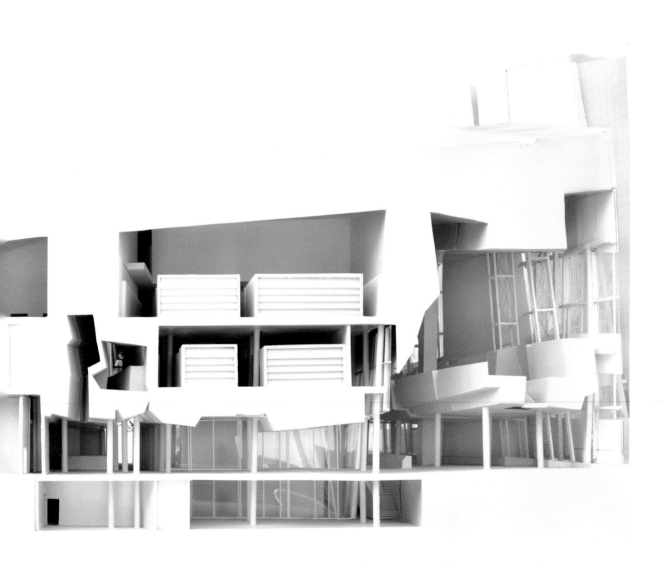

Cidade da Cultura de Galicia II 2010

JORGE LUIS BORGES

THE GARDEN OF FORKING PATHS

FICTIONS

JORGE LUIS BORGES

"El jardín de senderos que se bifurcan," 1941

Ficciones. Buenos Aires: Sur, 1944

ON PAGE 242 of Liddell Hart's *History of World War I* you will read that an attack against the Serre-Montauban line by thirteen British divisions (supported by 1,400 artillery pieces), planned for the 24th of July, 1916, had to be postponed until the morning of the 29th. The torrential rains, Captain Liddell Hart comments, caused this delay, an insignificant one, to be sure. The following statement, dictated, reread and signed by Dr. Yu Tsun, former professor of English at the *Hochschule* at Tsingtao, throws an unsuspected light over the whole affair. The first two pages of the document are missing.

"... and I hung up the receiver. Immediately afterwards, I recognised the voice that had answered in German. It was that of Captain Richard Madden. Madden's presence in Viktor Runeberg's apartment meant the end of our anxieties and—but this seemed, *or should have seemed*, very secondary to me—also the end of our lives. It meant that Runeberg had been arrested or murdered.[1] Before the sun set on that day, I would encounter the same fate. Madden was implacable. Or rather, he was obliged to be so. An Irishman at the service of England, a man accused of laxity and perhaps of treason, how could he fail to seize and be thankful for such a miraculous opportunity: the discovery, capture, maybe even the death of two agents of the German Reich? I went up to my room; absurdly I locked the door and threw myself on my back on the narrow iron cot. Through the window I saw the familiar roofs and the cloud-shaded six o'clock sun. It seemed incredible to me that that day without premonitions or symbols should be the one of my inexorable death. In spite of my dead father, in spite of having been a child in a symmetrical garden of Hai Feng, was I—now—going to die? Then I reflected that everything happens to a man precisely, precisely *now*. Centuries of centuries and only in the present do things happen; countless men in the air, on the face of the earth and the sea, and all that really is happening is happening to me... The almost intolerable recollection of Madden's horselike face banished these wanderings. In the midst of my hatred and terror (it means nothing to me now to speak of terror, now that I have mocked Richard Madden, now that my throat yearns for the noose) it occurred to me that tumultuous and doubles happy warrior did not suspect that I possessed the Secret. The name of the exact location of the new British artillery park on the River Ancre. A bird streaked across the grey sky and blindly I translated it into an airplane and that airplane into many (against the French sky) annihilating the artillery station with vertical bombs. If only my mouth, before a bullet shattered it, could cry out that secret name so it could be heard in Germany... My human voice was very weak. How might I make it carry to the ear of the Chief? To the ear of that sick and hateful man who knew nothing of Runeberg and me save that we were in Staffordshire and who was waiting in vain for our report in his arid office in Berlin, endlessly examining newspapers... I said out loud: *I must see*. I sat up noiselessly, in a useless perfection of silence, as if Madden were already lying in wait for me. Something—perhaps the mere vain ostentation of proving my resources were nil—made me look through my pockets. I found what I knew I would find. The American watch, the nickel chain and the square coin, the key ring with the

---

1 An hypothesis both hateful and odd. The Prussian spy Hans Rabener, alias Viktor Runeberg, attacked with drawn automatic the bearer of the warrant for his arrest, Captain Richard Madden. The latter, in self-defense, inflicted the wound which brought about Runeberg's death (Editor's note.)

incriminating useless keys to Runeberg's apartment, the notebook, a letter which I resolved to destroy immediately (and which I did not destroy), a crown, two shillings and a few pence, the red and blue pencil, the handkerchief, the revolver with one bullet. Absurdly, I took it in my hand and weighed it in order to inspire courage within myself. Vaguely I thought that a pistol report can be heard at a great distance. In ten minutes my plan was perfected. The telephone book listed the name of the only person capable of transmitting the message; he lived in a suburb of Fenton, less than a half-hour train ride away.

I am a cowardly man. I say it now, now that I have carried to its end a plan whose perilous nature no one can deny. I know its execution was terrible. I didn't do it for Germany, no. I care nothing for a barbarous country which imposed upon me the abjection of being a spy. Besides, I know of a man from England—a modest man—who for me is no less great than Goethe. I talked with him for scarcely an hour, but during that hour he was Goethe... I did it because I sensed that the Chief somehow feared people of my race—for the innumerable ancestors who merge within me. I wanted to prove to him that a yellow man could save his armies. Besides, I had to flee from Captain Madden. His hands and his voice could call at my door at any moment. I dressed silently, bade farewell to myself in the mirror, went downstairs, scrutinized the peaceful street and went out. The station was not far from my home, but I judged it wise to take a cab. I argued that in this way I ran less risk of being recognised; the fact is that in the deserted street I felt myself visible and vulnerable, infinitely so. I remember that I told the cab driver to stop a short distance before the main entrance. I got out with voluntary, almost painful slowness; I was going to the village of Ashgrove but I bought a ticket for a more distant station. The train left within a very few minutes, at eight-fifty. I hurried; the next one would leave at nine-thirty. There was hardly a soul on the platform. I went through the coaches; I remember a few farmers, a woman dressed in mourning, a young boy who was reading with fervor the *Annals* of Tacitus, a wounded and happy soldier. The coaches jerked forward at last. A man whom I recognised ran in vain to the end of the platform. It was Captain Richard Madden. Shattered, trembling, I shrank into the far corner of the seat, away from the dreaded window.

From this broken state I passed into an almost abject felicity. I told myself that the duel had already begun and that I had won the first encounter by frustrating, even if for forty minutes, even if by a stroke of fate, the attack of my adversary. I argued that this slightest of victories foreshadowed a total victory. I argued (no less fallaciously) that my cowardly felicity proved that I was a man capable of carrying out the adventure successfully. From this weakness I took strength that did not abandon me. I foresee that man will resign himself each day to more atrocious undertakings; soon there will be no one but warriors and brigands; I give them this counsel: *The author of an atrocious undertaking ought to imagine that he has already accomplished it, ought to impose upon himself a future as irrevocable as the past.* Thus I proceeded as my eyes of a man already dead registered the elapsing of that day, which was perhaps the last, and the diffusion of the night. The train ran gently along, amid ash trees. It stopped, almost in the middle of the fields. No one announced the name of the station. "Ashgrove?" I asked a few lads on the platform. "Ashgrove," they replied. I got off.

A lamp enlightened the platform but the faces of the boys were in shadow. One questioned me, "Are you going to Dr. Stephen Albert's house?" Without waiting for my answer, another said, "The house is a long way from here, but you won't get lost if you take this road to the left and at every crossroad turn again to your left." I tossed them a coin (my last), descended a few stone steps and started down the solitary road. It went downhill, slowly. It was of elemental earth; overhead the branches were tangled; the low, full moon seemed to accompany me. For an instant, I thought that Richard Madden in some way had penetrated my desperate plan. Very quickly, I understood that was impossible. The instructions to turn always to the left reminded me that such was the common procedure for discovering the central point of certain labyrinths. I have some understanding of labyrinths: not for nothing am I the great grandson of that Ts'ui Pên who was governor of Yunnan and who renounced worldly power in order to write a novel that might be even more populous than the *Hung Lu Meng* and to construct a labyrinth in which all men would become lost. Thirteen years he dedicated to these heterogeneous tasks, but the hand of a stranger murdered him—and his novel was incoherent and no one found the labyrinth. Beneath English trees I meditated on that lost maze: I imagined it inviolate and perfect at the secret crest of a mountain; I imagined it erased by rice fields or beneath the water; I imagined it infinite, no longer composed of octagonal kiosks and returning paths, but of rivers and provinces and kingdoms... I thought of a labyrinth of labyrinths, of one sinuous spreading labyrinth that would encompass the past and the future and in some way involve the stars. Absorbed in these illusory images, I forgot my destiny of one pursued. I felt myself to be, for an unknown period of time, an abstract perceiver of the world. The vague, living countryside, the moon, the remains of the day worked on me, as well as the slope of the road which eliminated any possibility of weariness. The afternoon was intimate, infinite. The road descended and forked among the now confused meadows. A high-pitched, almost syllabic music approached and receded in the shifting of the wind, dimmed by leaves and distance. I thought that a man can be an enemy of other men, of the moments of other men, but not of a country: not of fireflies, words, gardens, streams of water, sunsets. Thus I arrived before a tall, rusty gate. Between the iron bars I made out a poplar grove and a pavilion. I understood suddenly two things, the first trivial, the second almost unbelievable: the music came from the pavilion, and the music was Chinese. For precisely that reason I had openly accepted it without paying it any heed. I do not remember whether there was a bell or whether I knocked with my hand. The sparkling of the music continued. From the rear of the house within a lantern approached: a lantern that the trees sometimes striped and sometimes eclipsed, a paper lantern that had the form of a drum and the color of the moon. A tall man bore it. I didn't see his face for the light blinded me. He opened the door and said slowly, in my own language: "I see that the pious Hsi P'eng persists in correcting my solitude. You no doubt wish to see the garden?"

I recognised the name of one of our consuls and I replied, disconcerted, "The garden?"

"The garden of forking paths."

Something stirred in my memory and I uttered with incomprehensible certainty, "The garden of my ancestor Ts'ui Pên."

"Your ancestor? Your illustrious ancestor? Come in."

The damp path zigzagged like those of my childhood. We came to a library of Eastern and Western books. I recognised bound in yellow silk several volumes of the Lost Encyclopedia, edited by the Third Emperor of the Luminous Dynasty but never printed. The record on the phonograph revolved next to a bronze phoenix. I also recall a *famille rose* vase and another, many centuries older, of that shade of blue which our craftsmen copied from the potters of Persia...

Stephen Albert observed me with a smile. He was, as I have said, very tall, sharp-featured, with grey eyes and a grey beard. He told me that he had been a missionary in Tientsin "before aspiring to become a Sinologist."

We sat down—I on a long, low divan, he with his back to the window and a tall circular clock. I calculated that my pursuer, Richard Madden, could not arrive for at least an hour. My irrevocable determination could wait.

"An astounding fate, that of Ts'ui Pên," Stephen Albert said. "Governor of his native province, learned in astronomy, in astrology and in the tireless interpretation of the canonical books, chess player, famous poet and calligrapher—he abandoned all this in order to compose a book and a maze. He renounced the pleasures of both tyranny and justice, of his populous couch, of his banquets and even of erudition—all to close himself up for thirteen years in the Pavilion of the Limpid Solitude. When he died, his heirs found nothing save chaotic manuscripts. His family, as you may be aware, wished to condemn them to the fire; but his executor—a Taoist or Buddhist monk—insisted on their publication."

"We descendants of Ts'ui Pên," I replied, "continue to curse that monk. Their publication was senseless. The book is an indeterminate heap of contradictory drafts. I examined it once: in the third chapter the hero dies, in the fourth he is alive. As for the other undertaking of Ts'ui Pên, his labyrinth..."

"Here is Ts'ui Pên's labyrinth," he said, indicating a tall lacquered desk.

"An ivory labyrinth!" I exclaimed. "A minimum labyrinth."

"A labyrinth of symbols," he corrected. "An invisible labyrinth of time. To me, a barbarous Englishman, has been entrusted the revelation of this diaphanous mystery. After more than a hundred years, the details are irretrievable; but it is not hard to conjecture what happened. Ts'ui Pên must have said once: *I am withdrawing to write a book. And another time: I am withdrawing to construct a labyrinth.* Every one imagined two works; to no one did it occur that the book and the maze were one and the same thing. The Pavilion of the Limpid Solitude stood in the centre of a garden that was perhaps intricate; that circumstance could have suggested to the heirs a physical labyrinth. Ts'ui Pên died; no one in the vast territories that were his came upon the labyrinth; the confusion of the novel suggested to me that it was the maze. Two circumstances gave me the correct solution of the problem. One: the curious legend that Ts'ui Pên had planned to create a labyrinth which would be strictly infinite. The other: a fragment of a letter I discovered."

Albert rose. He turned his back on me for a moment; he opened a drawer of the black and gold desk. He faced me and in his hands he held a sheet of paper that had once been crimson, but was now pink and tenuous and cross-sectioned. The fame of Ts'ui Pên as a calligrapher had been justly won. I read, uncomprehendingly and with fervour, these words written with a minute brush by a man of my blood: *I leave to the various futures (not to all) my garden of forking paths.* Wordlessly, I returned the sheet. Albert continued:

"Before unearthing this letter, I had questioned myself about the ways in which a book can be infinite. I could think of nothing other than a cyclic volume, a circular one. A book whose last page was identical with the first, a book which had the possibility of continuing indefinitely. I remembered too that night which is at the middle of the *Thousand and One Nights* when Scheherazade (through a magical oversight of the copyist) begins to relate word for word the story of the Thousand and One Nights, establishing the risk of coming once again to the night when she must repeat it, and thus on to infinity. I imagined as well a Platonic hereditary work. transmitted from father to son, in which each new individual adds a chapter or corrects with pious care the pages of his elders. These conjectures diverted me; but none seemed to correspond, not even remotely, to the contradictory chapters of Ts'ui Pên. In the midst of this perplexity, I received from Oxford the manuscript you have examined. I lingered, naturally, on the sentence: *I leave to the various futures (not to all) my garden of forking paths*. Almost instantly, I understood: 'the garden of forking paths' was the chaotic novel; the phrase 'the various futures (not to all)' suggested to me the forking in time, not in space. A broad rereading of the work confirmed the theory. In all fictional works, each time a man is confronted with several alternatives, he chooses one and eliminates the others; in the fiction of Ts'ui Pên, he chooses—simultaneously—all of them. He creates, in this way, diverse futures, diverse times which themselves also proliferate and fork. Here, then, is the explanation of the novel's contradictions. Fang, let us say, has a secret; a stranger calls at his door; Fang resolves to kill him. Naturally, there are several possible outcomes: Fang can kill the intruder, the intruder can kill Fang, they both can escape, they both can die, and so forth. In the work of Ts'ui Pên, all possible outcomes occur; each one is the point of departure for other forkings. Sometimes, the paths of this labyrinth converge: for example, you arrive at this house, but in one of the possible pasts you are my enemy, in another, my friend. If you will resign yourself to my incurable pronunciation, we shall read a few pages."

His face, within the vivid circle of the lamplight, was unquestionably that of an old man, but with something unalterable about it, even immortal. He read with slow precision two versions of the same epic chapter. In the first, an army marches to a battle across a lonely mountain; the horror of the rocks and shadows makes the men undervalue their lives and they gain an easy victory. In the second, the same army traverses a palace where a great festival is taking place; the resplendent battle seems to them a continuation of the celebration and they win the victory. I listened with proper veneration to these ancient narratives, perhaps less admirable in themselves than the fact that they had been created by my blood and were being restored to me by a man of a remote empire, in the course of a desperate adventure, on a Western isle. I remember the last words, repeated in each version like a secret commandment: *Thus fought the heroes, tranquil their admirable hearts, violent their swords, resigned to kill and to die.*

From that moment on, I felt about me and within my dark body an invisible, intangible swarming. Not the swarming of the divergent, parallel and finally coalescent armies, but a more inaccessible, more intimate agitation that they in some manner prefigured. Stephen Albert continued:

"I don't believe that your illustrious ancestor played idly with these variations. I don't consider it credible that he would sacrifice thirteen years to the infinite execution of a rhetorical experiment. In your country, the novel is a subsidiary form of literature; in Ts'ui Pên's time it was a despicable form. Ts'ui Pên was a brilliant novelist, but he was also a man of letters who doubtless did not consider himself a mere novelist. The testimony of his contemporaries proclaims—and his life fully confirms—his metaphysical and mystical interests. Philosophic controversy usurps a good part of the novel. I know that of all problems, none disturbed him so greatly nor worked upon him so much as the abysmal problem of time. Now then, the latter is the only problem that does not figure in the pages of the *Garden*. He does not even use the word that signifies *time*. How do you explain this voluntary omission?"

I proposed several solutions—all unsatisfactory. We discussed them. Finally, Stephen Albert said to me:

"In a riddle whose answer is chess, what is the only prohibited word?"

I thought a moment and replied, "The word *chess*."

"Precisely," said Albert. "*The Garden of Forking Paths* is an enormous riddle, or parable, whose theme is time; this recondite cause prohibits its mention. To omit a word always, to resort to inept metaphors and obvious periphrases, is perhaps the most emphatic way of stressing it. That is the tortuous method preferred, in each of the meanderings of his indefatigable novel, by the oblique Ts'ui Pên. I have compared hundreds of manuscripts, I have corrected the errors that the negligence of the copyists has introduced, I have guessed the plan of this chaos, I have re-established—I believe I have re-established—the primordial organisation, I have translated the entire work: it is clear to me that not once does he employ the word 'time.' The explanation is obvious: *The Garden of Forking Paths* is an incomplete, but not false, image of the universe as Ts'ui Pên conceived it. In contrast to Newton and Schopenhauer, your ancestor did not believe in a uniform, absolute time. He believed in an infinite series of times, in a growing, dizzying net of divergent, convergent and parallel times. This network of times which approached one another, forked, broke off, or were unaware of one another for centuries, embraces *all* possibilities of time. We do not exist in the majority of these times; in some you exist, and not I; in others I, and not you; in others, both of us. In the present one, which a favourable fate has granted me, you have arrived at my house; in another, while crossing the garden, you found me dead; in still another, I utter these same words, but I am a mistake, a ghost."

"In every one," I pronounced, not without a tremble to my voice, "I am grateful to you and revere you for your re-creation of the garden of Ts'ui Pên."

"Not in all," he murmured with a smile. "Time forks perpetually toward innumerable futures. In one of them I am your enemy."

Once again I felt the swarming sensation of which I have spoken. It seemed to me that the humid garden that surrounded the house was infinitely saturated with invisible persons. Those persons were Albert and I, secret, busy and multiform in other dimensions of time. I raised my eyes and the tenuous nightmare dissolved. In the yellow and black garden there was only one man; but this man was as strong as a statue... this man was approaching along the path and he was Captain Richard Madden.

"The future already exists," I replied, "but I am your friend. Could I see the letter again?"

Albert rose. Standing tall, he opened the drawer of the tall desk; for the moment his back was to me. I had readied the revolver. I fired with extreme caution. Albert fell uncomplainingly, immediately. I swear his death was instantaneous—a lightning stroke.

The rest is unreal, insignificant. Madden broke in, arrested me. I have been condemned to the gallows. I have won out abominably; I have communicated to Berlin the secret name of the city they must attack. They bombed it yesterday; I read it in the same papers that offered to England the mystery of the learned Sinologist Stephen Albert who was murdered by a stranger, one Yu Tsun. The Chief had deciphered this mystery. He knew my problem was to indicate (through the uproar of the war) the city called Albert, and that I had found no other means to do so than to kill a man of that name. He does not know (no one can know) my innumerable contrition and weariness."

The Museums of the Future

Maxwell L. Anderson

This essay summarises how museums of the future must adapt to changing perspectives about the ownership, sponsorship and audience of and for cultural heritage. The traditional model of collecting institutions changed radically in the seventies, with new pressure to focus less on collecting than on the experience of the visitor. By the nineties, a commercial instinct began to define museums, yielding larger crowds but also confusion about the primary mission of what had heretofore been educational institutions. Today museums are becoming a contested field in which cultural property laws are becoming more restrictive, ethical prohibitions against collecting archaeological or ethnographic works are growing and claims for cultural property already in museums are on the rise. The needs for increased funding of facilities that grew greatly in size and complexity over the last generation are not being met. And the audiences being sought and served are becoming more demanding and more diverse. The museum of the future thus faces a paradox: even as these institutions have grown and become more central to the identity of society, a transitory, global audience interconnected by jet travel and the Internet is too vast and too disparate to serve as easily as before. Museums today are accordingly adapting to constantly changing rules of collecting, sources of funding and visitor profiles. And museums tomorrow will both need to reflect this changing social order and meet new expectations at a previously unimaginable pace. The challenges and opportunities for social relevance are both daunting and exhilarating.

1

THE ROSETTA-STONE IN THE BRITISH MUSEUM.

2

3

BEFORE THE ADVENT OF THE modern museum, multiple contexts for the experience of collections both private and public allowed artefacts to endure but rarely to be set into a context that the general public could appreciate. In the course of the twentieth century, advances on several fronts improved the professionalism of museums and shaped experimentation with the best kinds of programming and interpretation.

SOME OF THE IMPETUS FOR widespread change in the last quarter of the last century may be traced to student uprisings in the sixties throughout Europe and the United States, demanding a rejection of tradition for its own sake, greater social equality and the emergence of new models privileging the general population over the leadership class. There have followed a succession of approaches to the highly flexible mission of museums, from an educational thrust to service as community centres.

REGARDLESS OF THEIR PERCEIVED MANDATE in any given generation, museums have long occupied centre stage in the world's great cities. Examples include the Louvre in Paris, the British Museum in London, the Metropolitan Museum of Art in New York and the Prado in Madrid. In different ways, the profile of these institutions defines the character not just of their cities but also of their nations past and present. As the world shifts from rural to urban, the clustered collections, exhibitions and programmes of museums take on a larger role in shaping national dialogues about the definition and importance of cultural heritage, the state of our collective contribution to history and the larger context against which we may assess aspirations for societal benefit in the future.

NATIONALISM HAS BEEN A FACTOR in the growth of museums, but so has a more local manifestation of civic pride: regions and municipalities. In the Middle Ages it was essential to have a cathedral within the reach of pilgrims. The modern era's secular successor to cathedrals is museums. Like cathedrals, museums provide a large-scale landmark dedicated to the gathering of numerous people for a dedicated purpose. Most great cities have multiple museums, which have proliferated over the last century to swallow up the teeming population seeking a place to connect with others and with lasting attributes of society—such as the evidence of artistic or cultural heritage.

CIVIC PRIDE OVER THE PAST two decades has yielded the demand for a hybrid institution: part museum of the past and economic engine of the present. The pursuit of cultural centres that can serve a variety of purposes, from affirming the broader identity of a place to inducing residents and travellers to make it their own, to catalysing further investment in an area are all legitimate and worthwhile ambitions. But the core mandate of museums begins with building collections, caring for them and making them of interest to a broad public.

THIS ORIGINAL INTRINSIC MISSION HAS been sidelined over the last generation as a mad rush to make a city or region relevant through culture has become the primary driver of decision-making. Many have fallen prey to a trend to look at museums not as

4

5

6

4 Ted Sparrow helps to mount birds of his grandfather Thomas Sparrow's collection of some 1,500 birds from all over the world. 1933

5 Copyists at musèe du Louvre, Paris. 1947

6 The sculptures of the Parthenon on view at the Elgin gallery at The British Museum, London. 1949

treasure houses with much to teach us but as economic engines that have much to sell us. Blockbuster exhibitions, dating back to the *Treasures of Tutankhamen* in 1978, began to eclipse great permanent collections as the barometer of institutional relevance. The pursuit of crowds overtook the pursuit of art purchases and gifts as the proving ground for a museum's value, and the mainstream media began to report on exhibition attendance numbers as they do to opening weekend ticket sales of Hollywood movies. The result has been the creation of a reward system for museum administrators: if you bring in more visitors, you succeed. If, on the other hand, this year's number of visitors declines in relation to last year's, you have a problem that has to be solved.

THIS MIGHT MAKE SENSE IF the value of museums could be reduced to the value of the commercial film industry: success in that field is measured in financial terms, which is why televised award shows are so closely watched. A trophy for a critically successful movie can drive more ticket-buyers in a second wave of theatrical releases.

BUT NOT ALL MOTION PICTURES are created with the singular goal of making money, and museums were founded not as commercial establishments, or entertainment venues. They began as the repositories of national heritage, whether conceived as such from the outset or whether invented as such from the spoils of war, conquest or royal or noble collecting. And they are manifestly poor at monetising their collections and exhibitions—for good reason.

THE FINANCIAL AND REPUTABLE SUCCESS of the Guggenheim Bilbao in 1997 enshrined what had until then been an exhibition-focused story. The premise of the Guggenheim project was that capital investment in physical infrastructure was also investment in the promise of culture as an economic engine. This had not previously been advanced as an argument so forcefully or so successfully. But what emerged as a potential model has yet to repeat itself. The opening of London's Tate Modern in 2000 bears some resemblance—but there were critical differences. The Tate had already been for generations a London-based museum; it had a commitment to the art it would show in its new facility—which was not an architectural marvel but a colossal renovation of a liability: an abandoned power plant. The UK Lottery was a prime part of the ongoing funding strategy, rather than a direct government appropriation. And the overarching leader of the enterprise was a charismatic director in the home city of the Tate, not a remote museum with no previous ties to the Basque Region.

SO THE GUGGENHEIM BILBAO REMAINS, over thirteen years later, a unique example of "starchitecture" at its most risky—a formula for building facilities with no anchoring collection, no embedded curatorial team to support it and a leveraged, grafted on "brand" as the value proposition, rather than a resource that grew up organically in the city of Bilbao, as did the Museo de Bellas Artes.

7 Courtyard and Pyramids by I. M. Pei in musèe du Louvre, Paris. 1993

8 The British Museum, London. 2005

9 Museo del Prado, Madrid. 2006

But Guggenheim Bilbao helped spawn a building spree that is still playing out. The United Arab Emirates undertook a massive cultural complex in Abu Dhabi. Multiple museums began planning branches in the provinces, ultimately including the Louvre and the Pompidou. American museums undertook large-scale additions or new buildings, and China has spawned hundreds of museums over the last decade, many lacking adequate curatorial oversight.

So here we are, as the smoke begins to clear from a raging recession that has slowed but not stopped a building boom in museums, which provides an ideal opportunity to reflect on the museum of the future not just from the vantage point of government agencies, tourist bureaus, or corporate investors, but from the perspective of potential audiences and the professional staff who will be challenged to find sustainable ways of serving them that benefit the public interest.

We may begin, appropriately, with the goal of most museums: to collect. Museums have collected since they first appeared. However, the predicament for museums of the future with regard to collecting is this: multiple categories of man-made artefacts are no longer so simple to obtain. To begin with archaeological materials and ancient art, an emerging consensus since the 1970 UNESCO *Convention on the Means of Prohibiting and Preventing the Illicit Import, Export and Transfer of Ownership of Cultural Property* has all but dried up the purchase of artefacts lacking pre-1970 ownership histories. While some museums continue to accept gifts and bequests of material which has no clear title or export history, the vast majority of collecting institutions appears to have drawn a "bright line," according to which the value assigned to providing a home for objects is less than the value assigned to avoiding any actions that might encourage future tomb-robbing, destruction of ancient sites or associated crimes. The fact that the illicit trade in antiquities has been linked to the money laundering of terrorist cells and of organised crime has had a secondary but no less powerful chilling effect.

The resulting conundrum, however, is that every hour more artefacts are uncovered somewhere in the world, as public works projects and private development efforts continue without interruption. The excavation of land for commercial projects as well as for roads, railway lines and public works in general yields an immeasurable and unwelcome harvest: precious artefacts for which there is no simple solution or safe harbour. The storerooms of national and regional archaeological museums are often filled to capacity even without these so-called "chance" or stray finds. And the hasty excavation of such works to facilitate progress in construction and public works is likely to yield imperfect or largely unusable archaeological evidence.

Museums must find a way to come to an agreement with both private developers and those construction firms responsible for excavation to halt digging long enough for

10 Guggenheim, Bilbao. 2003

11 Tate Modern & London Millennium Footbridge, London. 2000

12 The MET~Metropolitan Museum of Art, New York. 1995

a trained, state-appointed archaeologist to inspect the situation at hand and make a determination as to whether a work permit should be temporarily suspended pending further review, or left in effect. The shortage of capable professionals, temptation to suppress or destroy evidence that might delay costly construction and the easy money to be had by illegal sale to a third party prepared to remove such examples of cultural heritage are all complicating factors with no easy remedy. Britain's 1996 Treasure Act, which rewards the reporting of stray finds, has served to slow the illicit excavation of sites according to some—while to others it has encouraged *amateur* archaeology with metal detectors and the consequent destruction of important information connected with the origin of artefacts.

MUSEUMS ARE THE ONLY PLACES where chance finds, objects lacking provenance and recovered stolen material can be transferred. Only a new international convention that harmonises national heritage statutes and international treaties can provide a coherent way forward. The private buyer through an interconnected art market is simply too porous and tempting a solution for those who would privilege profit over patrimony.

ANOTHER ISSUE THAT MUSEUMS ARE today struggling to resolve is the collection of works of ethnographic origin. These are artefacts that have an enduring religious or ritual significance for those in living cultures connected with historical heritage. While in the past a Western explorer or anthropologist may have obtained such objects through seizure, sale or barter, there is no clear justification today for the removal of heritage from any people who may legitimately connect objects and contexts with their ancestral origins. Over the last two generations the Western privileging of scientific or pseudo-scientific enquiry has clashed with the assertion of ownership rights by native peoples. And any one of the hundreds of thousands of examples of native cultural heritage in museums around the world today can be the catalyst for a claim that might engender years of research, debate or litigation. While the heritage of living cultures was once collected with the intention of learning about other societies, today it is a battleground of competing values touching on ethics, politics and the very definition of ownership versus possession. Museums require in this arena as well a clearer path to the future—one which respects the rights of people to assert claims on cultural heritage, but one which also simultaneously acts with responsibility in connection with vast collections already held in the galleries and storerooms of museums around the globe.

OWNERSHIP DISPUTES IN RECENT YEARS have not been limited to claims by nations or subsets of living cultures; the most contentious claims may also originate with private individuals. Such is the case with art works that were or may have been seized

13 *Winged Victory of Samothrace*. 2th century BC

14 Stored Sculpture at the Museo Archeologico Nazionale, Naples. 1995

14

by the Nazis in the years leading up to World War II and right up to the end of the war in 1945. Complicating the adjudication of claims is the almost total absence of reliable documentation, whether photographic or otherwise, that can corroborate the memories or suppositions of victims of the Holocaust and their families. Museums bear a special responsibility to thoroughly research collections, seeking circumstantial evidence about works that may have been the subject not just of seizure, but also of so-called "pressure" sales, i.e., sales hurriedly arranged in order to recoup losses occasioned by other kinds of losses at the hands of the Nazis, such as bank or property theft. The negotiation of settlements around objects implicated in the horrors of the Holocaust requires a lesser standard than do conventional claims. The overarching moral imperative to restore displaced works to their proper owners may not in every instance be provable "beyond a reasonable doubt," to cite the American standard of justice. The proof may only be strong circumstantial evidence, which many museums have chosen to honour notwithstanding no legal obligation to do so.

AS THE CRIMES OF THE twentieth century recede in time, so do the memories and evidence of them. This fact has propelled many museums in Europe and the United States to pursue an accelerated programme of research on potential gaps in the ownership history of objects. The tide may begin to turn when the children of the generation most directly affected are no longer living. But the moral imperative to do what is right should surely take precedence over what is expedient, provable and urgent.

CRIMES OF STATE DID NOT end with the Nazis, of course. Museum professionals around the world were confounded by the Taliban's detonation of the Bamyan Buddhas and the looting of Afghan treasures with the full knowledge and consent of warlords in control of Afghan territories. In parts of certain developing countries it is routine for the very authorities that are notionally in charge of protecting cultural heritage to be the source of the black market for such works. Museum officials should expect and demand responsible conduct from those who are vested with the protection of historical sites and museums in source countries. But all too often the military strategies of indigenous or occupying forces are disconnected from, or even explicitly at odds with the best interests of cultural heritage. Once again museums require an international convention that can promptly and efficiently interdict the destruction or looting of sites, monuments and museums that are jeopardised by corrupt officials or marauding state-sanctioned iconoclasts.

THE MUSEUMS OF THE FUTURE, as we have seen, will confront a multitude of dilemmas with regard to collecting evidence of the past, but the task of assembling evidence of contemporary cultural heritage is in some ways even more complicated and problematic, given the extensive reliance today on man-made materials. Whether great

15 *Bust of Nefertiti.*
C. 1340 BC

examples of twentieth and twenty-first century design, contemporary architecture made with untested materials or works of art created with acrylic paint, polyurethane foams or fugitive inks, there is no certainty they will last more than a few decades. The museums of the future will be coping with obsolescent materials, deteriorating ingredients and no track record of preservation methods that have stood the test of time.

THE "BORN DIGITAL" AGE PRESENTS its own particular set of issues. Many can remember the days when so-called 'floppy disks' were the means by which information made its way from maker to recipient, but over the last twenty years so many electronic platforms and operating systems have proliferated and become obsolete that it is hard for us to keep count. This much is certain: the archiving of information is becoming more of a burden as the amount of information explodes and the ways in which it is stored and exchanged moves from one technology to another. The museums of the future will have mounting difficulty in retaining records of the history of creativity. Our total reliance on computer chips and networks as the means by which information is stored carries with it unknown risks, including the erasure of an incalculable amount of human knowledge on a scale that makes the burning of the Library of Alexandria seem modest.

PAYING FOR THE NEEDS OF museums in the future is rapidly becoming a much-debated topic in public policy. While most of the world's museums rely on some kind of government support, there are new calls to have museums become more self-reliant —depending on private contributions and consumer spending. Just as it would be disastrous for unprepared universities to shift their reliance precipitously to the private sector, so it is a highly risky and unproven plan for museums. Those that do depend on private funding for the majority of support have found that creative freedom can be all too easily sacrificed for the goal of commercial success and that culture heritage concerns can quickly take a back seat to spectacle, merchandising and corporate entertaining. While these have their place in the public life of museums, they cannot replace large-scale underwriting from endowments or government support and should not be mistaken for more than a supplementary revenue stream.

FINALLY WE TURN TO AUDIENCES. In truth, the prognosis surrounding public participation in the museums of the future is not clear. While zealous marketing studies and consulting firm reports have long embraced building for its own sake, the depleted resources of governments have made such colossal projects a challenging inheritance. The city of Valencia is one of several in Spain that have made promising major investments in cultural infrastructure, including San Sebastian, as well as Madrid itself. There is a nervous air in many world capitals, cities and regions that have staked a major claim on expansive cultural complexes, like Shanghai and now Galicia. Counting on a potential audience from throughout Europe, the plans were hatched during a boom time.

16

17

18

DESPITE THE NERVOUS ANTICIPATION AS each project opens to the public, one potentially welcome factor seems not to have played explicitly into the expansion boom of the last decade of the twentieth century and first decade of the twenty-first: the emergence of a massive tourist market from a new Asian middle class. Both in sheer numbers and in the novelty of leisure travel as a feature of economic growth, some 30 million Indians and 100 million Chinese are believed to be a new marketplace for cultural tourism that has yet to make itself felt. As the world's natural resources, labour market and population growth have shown, the United States and Europe are not growing in productivity to the extent of Latin and South America, Asia and potentially, in one or more generations, MENA (Middle East/North Africa) followed by Sub-Saharan Africa.

EACH REGION WILL FUEL GROWTH in cultural tourism, followed by immigration, followed by intermarriage, followed by the dissipation of what has driven global culture for time immemorial: national boundaries. Over the last two decades, the United Nations estimates that some 214 million migrants have been making their way around the world. This represents a growth of almost 40% since 1990. With the commingling of people and the transportation advances that have yet to be invented, the churn of people who become cultural vagabonds will grow geometrically and the traditional us/them divides will crumble.

THIS SEA CHANGE IN HOW we define audiences will have a palpable effect on the relevance of cultural offerings for every major institution around the world. The case for each museum will need to be reinvented, and the value proposition of museums in general will have to adapt to a series of new realities. These include a multilingual rather than a monoglot audience. We should begin to plan for a massive infusion of first-time museum-goers, who have no frame of reference about what to expect or how to visit and we must plan new opportunities for elective spending by tens of millions of visitors/consumers who may anticipate no major difference between a museum and a theme park, civic attraction or other public space energised by curated displays.

THESE CHANGES WILL DEMAND NEW strategies both for how museums engage with potential audiences and how they operate within a professional sphere. The public engagement question will play out as the mass movement of audiences begins to take shape. The professional operations of museums will have to reflect both a substantial increase in audience and a highly differentiated series of assumptions about the role of museums in relation to formal and information education, the care of cultural heritage, the provision of experiences more lasting and integral to intellectual development than commercial destinations and new business models that entice, rather than coerce, consumer spending and sources of support from taxation, grants, subsidies and investments.

19 *Bāmiyān Buddha.*
C. 6th century

As we prepare for the mobilisation of new tourist audiences through economic opportunity in Asia and other parts of the developing world, museum professionals can be rethinking our traditional mandates in creative ways. Museums will remain treasure houses but now have the exciting mandate of constantly adapting to societal change, applying the best thinking to connect a collecting mandate with a public one and seeking to innovate in the face of unpredictable external pressures. While the road ahead is lined with potholes, brigands and wrong turns, it also promises to include rewarding vistas, new encounters and a potentially better destination for museums.

101

20 *Spatial Concept.*
Lucio Fontana, 1959

21 *Untitled (Petit Palais).*
Felix Gonzalez-Torres, 1992

22 *TH.2058*. Dominique
Gonzalez-Foerster, 2008

Susan Sontag

The Volcano Lover

~ A romance ~

Susan Sontag

"Part I, Chapter 2"

The Volcano Lover. A romance. New York: Picador, 1992

II

They had been married, and childless, for sixteen years.

If the Cavaliere, who like so many obsessive collectors was a natural bachelor, married the only child of a wealthy Pembrokeshire squire to finance the plitical career he embarked on alter ten time-serving years in military regalia, it was not a good reason. The House of Commons, four years representing a borough in Sussex in which he never set foot, turned out to offer no more scope for his distinctive talents than the army. A better reason: it had brought him Money to buy pictures. He also had something richer than money. Yielding to the necessity of marrying—somewhat against my inclination, he was to tell another impecunious younger son, his nephew, many years later—he had found what he called lasting comfort. On the day of their marriage Catherine locked a bracelet on her wrist contining some of his hair. She loved him abjectly but without selfpity. He developed the improbable but just reputation for being an uxorious husband. Time evaporates, money is always hended, comforts found where they were not expected, and excitement dug up in barren ground.

He can't know what we know about him. For us he is a piece of the past, austerely outlined in powdered wig and long elegant coat and buckled shoes, beaky profile cocked intelligently, looking, observing, firm in his detachment. Does he seem cold? He is simple managing, managing brilliantly. He is absorbed, entertained by what he sees—he has an important, if not front-rank, diplomatic posting abroad—and he keeps himself busy. His is the hyperactivity of the heroic depressive. He ferried himself past one vortex of melancholy alter another by means of an astonishing spread of enthusiasms.

He is interested in everything. And he lives ina place that for ser volume of curiosities —historical, natural, social—could hardly be surpassed. It was bigger than Rome, it was the wealthiest as well as the most populous city on the Italian peninsula and, after Paris, the second largest city on the European continent, it was the capital of natural disaster and it has the most indecorous, plebeian monarca, the best ices, the marriest loafers, the most vapid torpor, and, amont the younger aristocrats, the largest number of future Jacobins. Its incomparable bay was home to freakish fish as well as the usual bouty. It had streets paved with blocas of lava and, some miles, Hawai, the gruesomely intact remains, recently rediscovered, of two dead cities. Its opera house, the biggest in Italy, provided a continual ravishment of *castrati*, another local product of internacional renown. Its handsome, highly sexed aristocracy gathered in one another's masions at nightly card parties, misleadingly called *conversazioni*, which often did not breauk up until dawn. On the streets life piled up, extruded, overflowed. Certain court celebrations included the building in front of the royal palace of an artificial mountain festooned with meta, game, cakes, and fruit, whose dismatling by the ravenous mob, unleashed by a salvo of cannon, was applauded by the overfed from balcones. During the great famine of the spring of 1764, people went off to the baker's with lond knives incide their shirts for the killing and mailing hended to get a small ration of bread.

The Cavaliere arrived to take up his post in November of that year. The expiatory processions of women with crowns of thorns and crosses on their backs had passed and the pillaging mobs dishanded. The grandees and foreign diplomats had retrieved the silver that they had hidden in convents. The court, which had fled north sixteen miles to the colosal, grimly horizontal residence at Caserta, was back in the city's royal palace. The air intoxicated with smells of the sea and coffee and honeysuckle and excrement, animal and human, instead of corpses rotting by hundreds on the streets. The thirty thousand dead in the plague that followed the famine were buried, too. In the Hospital of the Incurables, the thousands dying of epidemia illness no longer starved to death first, at the rate of sixty or seventy a day. Foreing supplies of corn had brought back the aceptable level of destitution. The poor were again cavorting with tambourines and full-throated songs, but many had kept the long knives incide their shirts which they'd worn to scout for bread and now murdered each other more often for the ordinary, civil and now mudered each other more often for the ordinary, civil reasons. And the emaciated peasants who had converged on the city in the spring were lingering, breeding. Once again the *cuccagna* would be built, savagely dismantled, devoured. The Cavaliere presented his credentials to the thirteen-year-old King, and the regents, rented a sapcious three-story mansión commanding a Herat-stopping view of the bay and Capri and the quiescent volcano for, in local money, one hundred fifty pounds a year, and began organizing as much employment as posible for his quickened energies.

Living abroad facilitates treating life as a spectacle—it is one of the reasons that people of means move abroad. Where those stunned by the horror of the famine and the brutality and incompetente of the goverment's response saw unending inertia, lethargy, a hardened lava of ignorante, the Cavaliere saw a flor. The expatriate's dancing city is often the local reformer's or revolutionary's immobilized one, ill-governed, committed to injustice. Different distance, different cities. The Cavaliere had never been as active, as stimulated, as alive mentally. As pleasurably detached. In the churches, in the narrow, steep streets, at the court—so many performances here. Among the bay's eccentric marine life, he noted with delight (no rivalry between art and nature for this intrepid connoisseur) one fish with tiny feet, and evolutionary overachiver who nevertheless hadn't made it out of the water. The sun beat down relentlessly. He trod steaming, spongy ground that was hot beneath his shoes. And bony ground loaded with rifts of treasure.

The obligations of social life of which so many dutifully complain, the maintenance of a great household with some fifty servants, including several musicians, keep his expenses rising. His envoy's salary was hardly adequate for the lavish entertainments required to impose himself on the imagination of people who counted, a necessary part of his job; for the expectations of the painters on whom he bestows patronage; for the price of antiquities and pictures for which he must compete with a host of rival collectors. Of course he is eventually going to sell the best of what he buys—and he does. A gratifying symmetry, that collecting most things requires Money but then the things collected themselves turn into more money. Though money was the faintly disreputable, necessary byproduct of his passion, collecting was still a virile occupation: not merely recognizing but bestowing value on things, by including them in on's collection. It stemmed from a lordly sense of himself that Catherine—indeed, all but a very few women—could not have.

His reputation as a connoisseur and man of learning, his affability, the favor he came to enjoy at court, unmatched by any other of the envoys, had made the Cavaliere the city's leading foreign resident. It was to Catherine's credit that she was no courtier, that she was revolved by the antics of the King, a youth of stupefying coarseness, and by his snobbish, fertile, intelligent wife, who wielded most of the power. As it did him credit that he was able to amuse the King. There was no reason for Catherine to accompany him to the food-slinging banquets at the royal palace to which he was convened three or four times a week. He was never bored when with her; but he was also happy to be alone, out for whole days on the bay in his boat harpooning fish, when his head went quiet in the sun, or gazing at, reviewing, itemizing his treasures in his cool study or the storeroom, or looking throught the new books on ichthyology or electricity or ancient history that he had ordered from London. One never he was spared in his marriage, a wholly successful mariage—one in which all needs were satisfied that had been given permission to arise. There was no frustration, at least on his part, therefore no longing, no desire to be together as much as posible.

Hight-minded where he was cynical, ailing while he was robust, tender when he forgot to be, correct as her table settings for sixty—the amiable, not too plain, harpsichord-playing heiress he had married seemed to him pure wife, as far as he could imagine such a being. He relished the fact that everyone thought her admirable. Conscientiously dependent rather than weak, she was not lacking in self-confidence. Religión animated her; her dismay at his impiety sometimes made her seem commanding. Besides his own person and career, music was the principal interest they had in common. When Leopold Mozart and his prodigy son had visited the city two years ago Catherine had becomingly trembled as she sat down to play for them, and them performed as superbly as ever. At the weekly concerts given in the British envoy's mansion, to which all of local society aspired to be invited, the very people who most loudly talked and ate through every opera during the season fell silent. Catherine tamed them. The Cavaliere was an accomplished cellist and violinist—he had taken lessons from the great Giardini in London when he was twenty—but she was the better musician, he freely allowed. He liked having reasons to admire her. Even more than wanting to be admired, he liked admiring.

Though his imagination was reasonably lascivious, his blood, so he thought, was temperate. In that time men with his privileges were usually corpulent by their third or fourth decade. But the Cavaliere had not lost a jot of his young man's appetite for physical exertion. He worried about Catherine's delicate, unexercised constitution, to the point of sometimes being made uneasy by the ardor with which she welcomed his punctual embraces. There was little sexual heat between them. He didn't regret not taking a mistress, though —whatever others might make of the oddity. Occasionally, opportunity plumped itself down reside him; the heat rose; and he found himself reaching from moist palm to layered clothes, unhooking, untying, fingering, pushing. But the venture would leave him with no desire to continue; he was drawn to other kinds of acquisition, of posesión. That Catherine took no more than a benevolent interest in his collections was just as well, perhaps. It is natural for lovers of music to enjoy collaborating, playing together. Most unnatural to be a co-collector. One wants to possess (and be possessed) alone.

*

It is my nature to collect, he once told his wife.

"Picture-mad," a friend from his youth called him—one person's nature being another's idea of mandes; of immoderate desire.

As a child he collected coins, then automata, then musical instruments. Collecting expresses a free-floating desire that attaches and re-attaches itself—it is a succession of desires. The true collector is in the grip not of what is collected but of collecting. By his early twenties the Cavaliere had already formed and been forced to sell, in order to pay debts, several small collections paintings.

Upon arriving as envoy he started collecting anew. Within an hour on horseback, Pompeii and Herculaneum were being dug up, stripped, picked over, but everything the ignorant diggers unearthed was supposed to go straight to the storerooms in the nearby royal palace at Portici. He managed to purchase a large collection of Greek vases from a noble family in Rome to whom they had belonged for generations. To collect is to rescue things, valuable things, from neglect, form oblivion, of simple form the ignoble destiny of being in somenone else's collection rather than one's own. But buying a whole collection insted of chasing down one's quarry piece by piece—it was not an elegant move. Collecting is also a sport, and its difficulty is part of what gives it honor and zest. A true collector prefers not to acquire in bulk (any more than hunters want the game simple driven past them), is not fulfilled by collecting another's collection: mere acquiring or accumulating is not collecting. But the Cavaliere was impatient. There are not only inner needs and exigencias. And he wanted to get on with what would be but the first of his Neapolitan collections.

No one in England had been surprised that he continued to col lect paintings or went alter atiquities once he arrived in Naples. But his interest in the volcano displayed a new side of his nature. Being volcano-mad was madder than being picture-mad. Perhaps the sun had gone to his head, or the fabled laxity of the south. Then the passion was quickly rationalized as a scientific interest, and also an aesthetic one, for the eruption of a volcano could be called, stretching the term, beatiful. There was nothing odd in his evening with guests invited to view the spectacle from the terrace of his country villa near the mountain, like the moonviewing parties of courtiers in Heian Japan. What was odd was that he wanted to be even closer.

The Cavaliere had discovered in himself a taste for the mildly plutonian. He started by riding with one groom out to the sulphurous ground west of the city, and bathing naced in the lake in the cone of a submerged extinct volcano. Walking onto his terrace those first months to see in the distance the well-behaved mountain sitting under the sun might provoke a reverie about the calm that follows catastrophe. Its plume of white smoke, the occasioal rumblings and jets of seatm seemed *that* perennial, unthreatening. Eighteen thousand villagers in Torre del Greco had died in 1631, an eruption even more letal than the one in which Herculaneum and Pompeii were entombed and the scholarly admiral of the Roman fleet, the Elder Pliny, famously lost his life, but since then, nothing that could merit thename of disaster.

The mountain had to wake up and Stara spitting to get the full attention of this much-occupied, much-diverted man. And did so, the year alter he arrived. The vapors that drifted up from the summit thickened and grew. Then black smoke mixed with the steam clouds and at night the cone's halo was tinted red. Hitherto absorbed by the hunt for vases and what minor finds from the excavations he could illicitly lay his hands on, he began to clima the mountain and take notes. On his fourth clima, reaching the upper slope, he passed a six-foot hillock of sulphur that hadn't been there the week befote. On his next clima up the snow-covered mountain—it was November—the top of the hillock was emitting a blue flame. He drew closer, stood on tiptoe, then a noise like artillery fire above—behind?—gripped his heart and he leapt backward. Some forty yards higher, at the opening of the crater, a column of black smoke had shot up, followed by an arc of stones, one of which sank near him. Yes.

He was seeing something he had always imagined, always wanted to know.

When an actual eruption began in March of the following year, when a cloud in the shape of a colossal umbrella pine—exactly as described in the setter of Pliny's nephew to Tacitus— poured upward from the mountain, he was at home practicing the cello. Watching from the roof that night, he saw the smoke go flame-red. A few days later there was a thunderous explosion and a gush of red-hot rocks, and that evening at seven o'clock lava began to boil over the top, coursing toward Portici. Taking with him only valet, groom, and local guide, he left the city on horseback and remained all night on the flank of the mountain. Hissing liquid metal on which fiery cinders floeated like boats cascaded past him a mere twenty yards away. He experience himself as fearless, always an agreeable illusion. Dawn rose and he started down. A mile below he caught up with the front of the lave stream, which had pooled in a deep hollow and been stopped.

From then on, the mountain was never free of its smoking wreath, the ocasional toss of blazing scoriae, the spurt of fire, the dribble of lava. And now he know what to do whenever he climbed the mountain. He gathered specimens of cooling lava in a leather pouch lined with lead, he bottled simples of the salts and sulphurs (deep yellow, red, orange) that he fetched from scorchingly hot cervices in the crater top. With the Cavaliere any passion sought the form of, was justified by becoming, a collection. (Soon other people were taking away pieces of the newly interesting volcano, on their one climb up; but accumulating souvenirs is not collecting.) This was pure collecting, short of the prospect of profit. Nothing to buy or sell here. Of the volcano he could only make a gift, to his glory and the glory of the volcano.

Fire again appeared at the top: a much more violent display of the mountain's energies was preaparing. It grumbled, rattled, and hissed; its emissions of stones more than once obliged even this hardiest of observers to quit the summit. When a great eruption took place the following year, the first full-scale eruption since 1631, he had more booty, a collection of volcanic rocks large and varied enough to be worth presenting to the British Museum, which he shipped back at his own expense. Collecting the volcano was his disinterested passion.

Naples had been added to the Grand Tour, and everybody who came hoped to marvel at the dead cities under the guidance of the learned British envoy. Now that the mountain had shown itself capable of being dangerous again, they wanted to have the great, terrifying experience. It had become another attraction and creator of employment for the ever needy: guides, litter bearers, porters, furnishers of victuals, grooms, and lantern carriers if the ascent was made at night—the best time to see the worst. Anything but impregnable by the standards of real mountains like the Alps, or even of Mount Etna, almost three times as high Vesuvius offered at most an exertion, sport only for *amateurs*. The exterminador could be mounted by anyone. For the Cavaliere the volcano was a familiar. He did not find the ascent very strenuous nor the dangers too frightening, whereas most people, underestimating the effort, were appalled by its arduousness, frightened by its vision of injury. Upon their return he would hear the stories of the great risks they had run, of the girandoles of fire, the hail (or shower) of stones, the accompanying racket (cannon, thunder), the infernal, mephitic, sulphurous stench. The very mouth of hell, that's what it is! So people believe it to be here, he would say. Oh, I don't mean literally, the visitor (if English, therefore usually Protestant) would reply.

Yet even as he wished for the volcano not to be profaned by the wheezing, the overweight, and the self-congratulatory, he longed—like any collector—to exhibit it. And was obliged to do so, if the visitor was a fired or relation from England or a foreign dignitary, as long as Vesuvius continued to flaunt its expressiveness. It was expected that he would chaperone an ascent. His eccentric friend from school days at Westminster, Frederick Hervey, about to be made a bishop, came for a long month; he took him up on an Easter Sunday, and Hervey's arm was seared by a moresel of volcanic effluvia; the Cavaliere supposed that he would be boasting about it for the rest of his life.

Hard to imagine that one could feel proprietary about this legendary menace, double-humped, some five thousand feet tall and eight miles from the city, exponed to the view of everyone, indeed the signatura feature of the local landscape. No object could be less ownable. Few natural wonders were more famous. Foreign painters were flocking to Naples: the volcano had many admirers. He set about, by the quality of his attentions, to make if his. He though about it more than anyone elese. My dear mountain. A mountain for a beloved? A monster? With the vases of the paintings or the coins or the statues, he could count on certain convencional recognitions. This passion was about what always surprised, alarmed; what exceded all expectations; and what never evoked the response that the Cavaliere wanted. But then, the obsessed collector, the appreciatons of other people always seen off-key, withholding, never appreciative enough.

*

Collections unite. Collection isolate.

They unite those who love the same thing. (But no one loves the same as I do; enough.) They isolate from those who don't share the passion. (Alas, almost everyone.)

Then I'll try not to talk about what interests me most. I'll talk about what insterests you. But this will remind me, often, of waht I can't share with you.

Oh, listen. Don't you see. Don't you see how beatiful it is.

*

It is not clear whether he was a natural teacher, an explainer (nobody did the tour of Pompeii and Herculaneum better), or learned to be one because so many people he was close to were younger than he and few were as cultivated. Indeed, it was the Cavaliere's destiny to have all the important relations of his life, counting or not counting Catherine, whith people much younger than himself. (Catherine was the only predictably younger person, by eight years: a wife is expected to be her husband's junior.) The royal playmate of his childhood had been seven and a half years his junior; the King of Naples was younger by twenty-one years. Younger people were drawn to the Cavaliere. He always seemed so interested in them, in furthering their talents, whatever these might be; so self-sufficient. Avuncular rather than paternal—he had never wanted to have children—he could be concerned, even responsable, without expecting too much.

Charles, his sister Elizabeth's son, was twenty when he arrived for the southermost stop on his Grand Tour. The pale self-assured little boy whom the Cavaliere had glimpsed a few times had become a highly intelligent, rather disablingly fastidious young man, with a modest, prudent, trove of pictures and objects of virtu and an extravagant collection of precious stones and minerals. He wanted to impress his uncle and he did. The Cavaliere recognized the abstracted, wandering, tensely amiable look of the collector—mineralogy was to be the ruling passion of Charles's life—and took an immediate living to him. Dutiful in the pursuit of entertainment, Charles procured the sexual services of a local courtesan named

cxvii

Madama Tschudi (distantly related to the harpsichord-making family), sat through a few evenings at the opera in his uncle's box, bouth ices and watermelon from the vendors on the Toledo, and avowed that he found Naples neither charming nor picturesque but squalid, boring, and dirty. He listened devoutly to his aunt at the harpsichord (Kuhnau, Royer, Couperin). He inspected with envy his uncle's hoard of paintings, statues, and vases; but rough lumps of tufa with pieces of lava or marine shells embedded in them, the framents of a volcanic bomb, or the bright yellow and orange salts he was shown only made him think with passion of his crystalized rubies, aspires, emeralds, diamonds—these could be called beatiful. He wahsed his hands often. And he resolutely refused to climb the mountain.

A formidable thought benevolent uncle would be too intimidating without some large eccentricity that made one feel a little protective. Declining the Cavaliere's second invitation to accompany him on a climb, Charles pleaded an intestinal weakness, the lack of a taste for danger. He hoped it would be taken as flattering rather than impertinent if he invoked the obvious classical allusion (many of the Cavaliere's friends in England made it): Remenber, I shouldn't like to hear that you've suffered the fate of the Elder Pliny. And now the Cavaliere, having just acquired a favorite nephew, could return the compliment: Then you shall be the Younger Pliny and report my death to the world.

*

Then as now an ascent had several stages. The road, in our own century turned into a motorway, did not exists then. But there was already a trail on which one came about two-thirds of the Mount Somma. This valley, now carpeted with black lava from the 1944 eruption, had trees, bramble, and high grasses. There the horses were left to graze while the volcano pilgrims continued up to the crater of foot.

Having left his horse with a groom, grasping his walking stick, pouch slung over one shoulder, the Cavaliere marched frimly up the slope. The point is to get a good rhythm, to make it mindless, almost as in a daydream. To walk like breathing. To make it what the body wants, what the air wants, what the time wants. And that is happening this morning, early morning on this occasion, except for the cold, except for the pain in his eras, from which his broad hat doesn't protect him. For the work of mindlessness there should not be any pain. He passed through the trees (a century ealier the slopes had been thik with forests and teeming with game), and beyond the tree line, where the wind cut more sharply. The trail darkened, steepened, past traces of black lava and rises of volcanic boulders. It began to feel like climbing now, his stride slowed, the stretch of muscles became preasantly perceptible. He didn't have to stop to match his breath but he did halt several times to scan the reddish-brown ground, looking for the spiky rocks with seams of color.

The ground turned grey, loose, quaggy—hindering, by yielding to, every step. The wind pushed against his head. Nearing the top, his ears hurt so much he stuffed them with wax.

cxviii

Reaching the boulder-rimmed summit, he paused and rubbed his sofa, icy eras. He gazed out and down at the iridescent blue skin of the bay. Then he turned. He never approached the crater without apprehension—partly the fear of danger, partly the fear of disappointment. If the mountain spat fire, hurled itself into the air, turned to flame and a moving wall of ash, that was an invitation to look. The mountain was exhibiting itself. But when the mountain was relatively quiet as it has been for several months, when it invited a closer look, he was looking for something new as well as checking to see that everything is the same. The prying look wishes to be rewarded. Even in the most pacified souls the volcano inspires a lust to see destructiveness.

He scrambled to the top of the cone and looked down. The vast hole, hundreds of feet deep, was still abrim with early-morning fog. He took the hammer from his pouch and looked about for a layer of color in the edge of the chasm. The fog was lifting as the sun warmed the air. With each gust of clarifying wind the view dropped farther and farther, without disclosing any fire. Dirty white jets of steam drifted upward from fissures in the lengthening crater walls. The burning innermost core lay hidden below the crust of slag. Not a glimmer. Pure massiveness—grey, inert. The Cavaliere sighed, and put his hammer back in the pouch. Inorganic matter makes a very melancholy impression on us.

Maybe it is not the destructiveness of the volcano that pleases most, though everyone loves a conflagration, but its defiance of the law of gravity to which every inorganic mass is subject. What pleases first at the sight of the plant world is its vertical upward direction. That is why we love trees. Perhaps we attend to a volcano for its elevation, like ballet. How high the molten rocks soar, how far above the mushrooming cloud. The thrill is that the mountain blows itself up, even if it must then like the dancer return to earth; even if it does not simple descend—it falls, falls on us. But first it goes up, it flies. Whereas everythin pulls, drags down. Down.

Cultural Palaces

The Role and Remaking of Metropolitan Arts Centres

Rachel Healy

In the sixties and seventies, art centres were a ubiquitous presence in the urban landscape. A creation of urban planners and bureaucrats, these monolithic structures provided a rarefied environment for experiencing the performing arts, with programming that privileged heritage art forms and conventional means of engagement with audiences. Three decades later, arts centres are continuing to flourish across Asia and throughout the developed world but many are now reinventing their physical environment, re-imagining their programming and reconnecting with new, younger audiences. These changes have occurred as a result of new programmatic contexts for presenting work, the creation of more holistic site-wide platforms for social interaction and the emancipation of popular culture artists and events within the programming mix.

"This is the way we wash our hands,"
"Wash our hands,"
"Wash our hands"
"This is the way we wash our hands"
"With PEARS' SOAP in the morning."

1 Intent boy watching movie in theater. 1947

2 *Pears' Soap* [press advertisement]. The Graphic, 1888

3 Soda jerk holding ice cream cone. 1950

How many of us remember feeling as children that arts centres were entirely inhabited by really old people? The smell of *Pears* soap and face powder, the audience dressed in their Sunday best, the angry glares from a parent or school teacher accompanied by a hushed reprimand not to kick the seat in front; the darkness; the interval queue in the loo and the crowd at the bar which would hopefully return a parent with a Cornetto ice-cream, the requirement to stay quiet—and then clap on demand, and continue clapping until hands ached while the actors feigned modesty and leaned heavily as they bowed.

123

At worst, arts centres of the past were also architectural eyesores, glorified car parks, slow moving and burdened with leaden programming, supportive of heritage art forms but slow to engage with new art forms and new audiences, frequently conformist, bureaucratic and trapped by the accoutrements of an earlier era: faux grandiosity in the form of red velvet and gold interiors; air-conditioned and lifeless. They were wholly prescriptive of the way audiences engage with the arts and intolerant of alternative ways in which artists and audiences might make connections. At worst, they also became a coded, self-congratulatory expression of achievement exclusively for the affluent and educated, dominated by traditions and rituals that straitjacket the relationship between artist and audience and that precluded engagement by the uninitiated.

But in spite of their failings they did offer a dedicated physical environment frequently in the geographical heart of their city for live performance. Unlike other art forms that can be experienced in solitude, live performance promises the thrill of a group of people agreeing to watch something together, as a community. While many experiences in life are improved by having fewer people around—an aeroplane flight, a visit to the supermarket, a ride in a lift—the performing arts are immeasurably enhanced by being in a theatre space that is full to capacity. Rather than inspiring a sense of dread, a "sold out" poster heightens a sense of excitement and anticipation among its community of ticket buyers. Whereas it is now possible to experience the performing arts through digital channels, the sweat and smell of an audience turns out to be an essential component of the experience for the individual attendees. Rituals that can be confusing and isolating for the uninitiated are also the backbone of the shared experience, a means by which an audience releases an energy that is greater than the sum of its parts. How many of us have been part of an audience in which some extraordinary alchemy occurs between artist and audience which moves the experience out of the everyday and can never again be repeated in quite the same way? For many of us who work in the theatre and attend technical and dress rehearsals, what can be ragged, chaotic and ill prepared in a rehearsal somehow ripens before an audience's gaze to create a transcendent magic. Participation in live performance

4 Crowded Opera Hall in the 71st opening of The Metropolitan Opera, New York. 1955

5 Mrs. Frank C. Henderson looking through her opera glasses. 1934

6 Whitestone Bridge Drive-In movie theater, New York. 1951

as an audience member or performer can be an almost primal pleasure and even in the restrained atmosphere of an arts complex of the seventies, the experience of witnessing live performance still resonated.

So why have arts centres survived and proliferated across the developed world? What are the contemporary challenges that accompany their architectural inheritance and how are new programming approaches helping to state the value of the arts centre to a new generation of cultural consumers as well as to the artists that animate its spaces? This essay attempts to address these issues and how arts centres are trying to find new ways of negotiating that essential relationship between artist and audience in a manner that energetically cultivates a bond between the two parties.

Unlike the relationship between an author or visual artist and their audience, performing arts practitioners usually have their work mediated by the architecture and traditions of the theatre or arts centre in which they perform. The opportunity to create an architectural expression of human creativity as well as provide a utilitarian and flexible home for the creation and delivery of live performance can be a challenge for architects: the developed world is crammed with cultural centres that are edifices, oversized and architecturally grand but cold and austere for the communities that inhabit them and the activities that will animate them. An ongoing challenge for arts programmers in these centres is to break through a lofty architectural heritage and create a space that deftly services its utilitarian and audience needs.

Often, the best theatres feel almost womb-like, intimate. The dynamics of the space, the distance and spatial relationship between the audience and the stage, the seating capacity, height of the auditorium, wing space, *proscenium* and acoustic all participate in the delivery of the performance and the sense of connection between artist and audience. In the best theatres, like the Belvoir Street Theatre in Sydney, the sense of communion is palpable. It is extraordinary to witness how the same touring show (or concert) can change so profoundly in accordance with the unique architectural and physical idiosyncrasies of each venue on its tour. Venues that fail to create a sense of intimacy with the artist on stage, or fail to create appropriate acoustics for the performance create huge challenges for programming staff and presenters in assuring audiences of the quality of the experience.

Aside from an architectural inheritance that may be unsympathetic or ignorant of the right kind of physical environment in which the relationship between artist and audience may thrive, programmers in arts centres today face an additional challenge. As arts centres worldwide broaden their mission to cater to multiple communities and audiences, aspiring not only to be centres of cultural engagement but also act as town squares or community gathering places, the need for a flexible and responsive

7 Frank Sinatra's fans waiting outside theater. 1943

8 Frank Sinatra singing. 1978

physical environment intensifies. As boundaries between art forms blur and artists experiment with new technologies in their work, as "high" and "low" are assimilated into the slipstream of popular culture, as arts centres are democratised and embrace contemporary popular culture in its infinite performative dimensions—comedy, cabaret, queer culture, screen, public lectures, burlesque, DJ/VJ events, baby discos, visual art installations and exhibitions, to name but a few—the hard edges of the physical environment and limitations of inherited resources are constantly challenged. The physical resources of such centres are almost always playing catch-up. Simultaneously, expectations concerning the digital transmission of performances increase, requiring enabling infrastructures to be built into the world's concert halls and theatres. The traditional concert hall, originally designed to host symphonic music, must now be equally adept at providing acoustic support for amplified music in every contemporary genre—electronica, jazz, pop, "world music," metal and rock all require most existing concert halls to not only retro-fit an acoustic treatment that supports the work of these artists but reconfigure the space so that a physical environment and ambience made to order can be created that is appropriate for that artist. The Sydney Opera House recently presented electronica legend Moby in its barn-like 2500-seat concert hall (like many concert halls, it was originally designed to present symphonic music). With a great lighting design, the intimacy and pulse of clubs could be effectively mimicked and ongoing experimentation with acoustic draping has improved the acoustics of the hall immeasurably. Notwithstanding, the pushing and pulling of a venue to create new made-to-order environments for performance requires continuing creativity, patience, flexibility and financing.

BEYOND THE PERFORMANCE SPACE, THE best foyers foster a sense of anticipation by virtue of being enclosed, cut off from "real" life. They become gathering places where performances are anticipated and then make a virtue of the audience's shared experience by encouraging social engagement at the foyer bar or in the area. Most festivals understand the importance of post-show drinking and social engagement and create or enlist local bars and supper clubs to extend their operating hours so that the audience experience may continue beyond the performance time, adding additional value to their evening. Smarter festivals understand that the performance is only one aspect of what makes a great evening (particularly for young audiences) and dedicate equal care and attention to developing "ancillary" activities—pre and post-show bars and supper clubs, free on-site entertainment, night markets and cafés, encouragement of post-show "tweets" and on-line reviews. Alas, some arts centres have still to admit that their responsibility to audiences extends beyond programming individual performance events to tailoring experiences that deliver the full social, intellectual and financial value from live

9 David Bowie performing during his tour *Serious Moonlight*. 1983

performances, making sense of their communal nature. Others, however, are increasingly shouldering responsibility for area planning and supporting cultural and commercial offerings (including food and beverage services and retail) so that audiences are offered more holistic leisure and entertainment options. While the impulse for this change in approach is often commercial reward, it makes sense of the fact that attending a performing arts event is a decision to participate in a community gathering and creating social platforms that respond to this experience is an obvious and critical part of the offering.

THESE CHANGES ARE SYMPTOMATIC OF a shift in the relationship between arts centres and their audiences and more sophisticated programming strategies, and it is worth considering how such centres have reinvented their role and civic purpose, as well as the content and context of their arts programmes.

OVER THE LAST TWO DECADES, many arts centres around the world have reconsidered their role within their communities and have shifted from passive "landlords" to impresarios: the role of administering a "hall for hire" has morphed into that of proactively producing and presenting work in its own right, thereby broadening the range of art forms presented, the demographics of audiences and the opportunities for digital engagement. Cloistered halls presenting largely classical repertoire and a management focused on activity within four walls have broadened to include programming a much wider range of cultural events (including "popular" culture events) both within and outside the traditional four walls.

THE DECISION MADE BY MANY arts centres around the world to actively programme and thereby curate performance seasons has produced myriad challenges. Relationships with resident companies have been rewritten so that the needs of the hirers do not exclusively dominate the planning and priority settings of arts centres. The historical users of the arts centres are being forced to make way for another major hirer—the actual "landlord." This has inevitably created tension as organisations accustomed to an operational relationship in which its preferred dates and access to venues are prioritised are now forced to negotiate access to the venues and their resources on new terms and conditions. And as competition for the ticket-buyer's entertainment dollar intensifies, it has been easy to see arts centres as aggressive new competitors rather than the benign hosts they used to be considered. Despite such challenges, these changes have also provided new opportunities for creative and business partnerships and collaboration and for broadening the performing arts' traditional attendance base through shared audience development initiatives. But perhaps more importantly, new and existing audiences have become the prime beneficiaries, as popular forms of cultural expression such as rap, comedy or queer

10

11

10 *Cats* billboard over Winter Garden
Theater, New York. 1989

11 Roman theatre ruins, Sabratha.
C. 180 AC

culture have not only been validated but also celebrated in the traditional temples of high art. Finally, the re-evaluation of artists working in these forms, which has positioned them as credible arts leaders, helps build the centres' ongoing relevance and credibility for new audiences and new generations.

THE GOAL OF THE SYDNEY Opera House is to present high quality and innovative Australian and international performing arts, providing opportunities for new and existing audiences to participate in and enjoy the opera house, to deliver a balanced, contemporary and original programme through proactively curating, producing, hosting and facilitating diverse commercial and non-commercial performance-related activities, deploying a range of tactics including commissioning, strategic business associations and collaborations, residency programmes and promotional positioning. It currently stages around 150 individual shows per year, almost half the shows presented across the theatre's seven unique performing spaces.

WITH THIS IN MIND, IT has proved critical at the Sydney Opera House to create and disseminate an artistic vision and a set of art form priorities and to gather a team of leaders in individual artistic disciplines who were responsible for particular art forms that represented five key areas: music, theatre and dance, contemporary culture, public programmes and education, and young audiences. Other centres have fewer artistic leadership roles commensurate with their overall artistic vision, strategy and activity level and do not engage artistic specialists from particular genres, but frequently engage instead a "generalist" artistic director.

THE HEADS OF THE VARIOUS sections at the Sydney Opera House are positioned, both internally and externally, as experts in their fields, connoisseurs of international trends and developments and outwardly focused champions of artists and their disciplines. Recruiting such expertise provides the organisation with an opportunity to develop a more sophisticated and layered conversation with audiences, one that over time engenders loyalty and trust in the curators' knowledge and selection of shows. Such a model learns from the success of a number of felicitous festival directors over the last four decades, particularly those who have built an unusually high level of reliability and trust among their communities. Fanny Mickey, long-standing artistic director of the Latin American Theatre Festival in Bogotá, Colombia, Claude Nobs, founder and continuing chief executive officer of the Montreux Jazz Festival in Switzerland, and Fergus Linehan, recently appointed artistic director of the Sydney Festival in Australia are all instructive examples of how single personalities can be completely embraced by their cities and how their organisations succeed in attracting high levels of attendance, media attention, business investment and critical praise for the events they programme and the artists they sponsor. In each instance, the director's

12

13

12 Teatro alla Scala, Milan. Giuseppe
Piermarini, 1776–1778

13 Donmar Warehouse Theatre, London.
1977

programming choices reflected an early understanding of the cultural tastes and popular preferences of the city and its diverse audiences, but in each of these three cases they also supported the community's trust and loyalty with inspiring work, inviting them to discover new art forms, challenging them with experimental or non-mainstream artists—in short, encouraging them to spend precious entertainment dollars on those original and game-changing artists that imagine new ways of seeing the world and ourselves. In an environment in which the supply of cultural commodities massively outstrips demand and a surfeit of entertainment, leisure, cultural and recreational opportunities compete with each other for consumer attention, hiring a reliable and trustworthy programming head (supported by an ongoing media and community profile) is proving to be a critical way of building audiences and maintaining their ticket-buying loyalty and sense of connection to the arts centre itself.

ONE OF THE DANGERS ENTAILED by this model is that too great an affiliation with a single personality renders the organisation vulnerable when the director in question leaves. As it is in any theatre or dance company that builds its reputation on the work of a single, charismatic artistic chief, succession planning is a prime concern, alongside an agreed set of programming priorities regarding the kind of artists and events the organisation selects. An arts organisation with a large number of internal and external stakeholders often requires a high standard of transparency around programming choices and traditionally "intuitive" programming processes are now carefully codified to ensure there is no uncertainty around the definition of ubiquitous terms like "excellence" or "innovation" and how choices are made. The purpose of this process is to build trust and understanding of an organisation's programming direction and to establish a reliable and formal framework by which individual events might be critically assessed. This approach helps build coherence across the content selection in all disciplines and programme choices consistent with the organisation's overarching artistic vision. It also allows an organisation to clarify its distinct role locally, nationally and internationally.

AS AN EXAMPLE, THE SYDNEY Opera House is a unique performing arts theatre and the de facto national performing arts centre, one of the most iconic buildings of the twentieth century and the emblem of a nation. It identified five key programming priorities (under the headings "old masters," "generational leaders," "new voices," "significant Australian and indigenous work" and "community") as well as definitions for each priority with a rationale that identified how the Sydney Opera House attained its iconic status through its programming decisions. These priorities provided a coherent reasoning and a cohesive artistic framework for artists as seemingly diverse as the Wiener Philharmoniker, theatre director Robert Lepage, forerunner of

14

15

14 Model stage set for Richard Wagner *Tannhauser*. Kurt Sohnlein, 1988

15 Isabella Rossellini at *Persephone* rehearsals in Teatro di San Carlo, Naples. 2001

electronica Moby, Aboriginal singer Geoffrey Gurrumul Yunipingu and a local choir comprising survivors of poverty, abuse and homelessness, The Choir of Hard Knocks. Other arts centres have identified a range of other key priorities (such as support for emerging artists, outreach support for cultural initiatives in the community) arising from their economic circumstances, artistic aspirations or individual community or government expectations. The priorities of the Sydney Opera House were not established by order of importance, nor did the organisation determine an annual quota for each priority area listed. However, as a unified set, they became a useful and consistent point of reference during the programme development process, and a part of an annual review of the organisation's direction and trends.

WHEN DEVELOPING PROGRAMMES, THE RESPONSIBILITY for creating an appropriate context for the presentation of an artist's work is fundamental to ensuring that an arts organisation is able to successfully foster a relationship between artist and audience. Creating the right context in which to present art work is one of the critical ongoing challenges facing arts centres and similar organisations worldwide, and it is a particular challenge for those organisations that do not have a subscription or membership programme (as these provide a base audience and box-office revenues). While it is easy for events that feature artists from popular culture to attract audiences, presenting new work or work by major artists who are unknown in local communities entails unique challenges. Given the right context, seasons sell out, artistic careers are launched or enhanced and organisations reap considerable benefits, both in financial terms and as regards their reputation. If an event is hosted in an inappropriate or misapprehended context, or indeed if it stands alone with no surrounding context, there is every chance that it will struggle to meet financial and organisational goals, irrespective of the artist's stature or the quality of the work. In Australia, performances by some of the world's most celebrated artists programmed at festivals have sold out, generating a great deal of media and public buzz before travelling to other cities, outside of a festival context, where they were welcomed by half-empty houses. Occasionally, community and media buzz can be generated in the course of the season itself but there are many more examples in which the seasons are too short to take advantage of late word-of-mouth and important and influential artists perform before a very small number of "insiders."

IN THE UNITED KINGDOM, THE Southbank's annual Meltdown Festival (which was first held in 1994) obtained a high level of audience and media attention by inventing a contemporary music festival that would be curated each year by a different high-profile musician from the field of popular culture. Festival directors have included David Bowie, Massive Attack, Patti Smith and Ornette Coleman and each one has programmed

16 Dancers of the Bolshoi Ballet warm up on the backstage before the performance at Bolshoi Theatre of Russia, Moscow. 1981

17 British director Peter Brook directs a rehearsal of his play *Mahabharata* at Theatre des Bouffes du Nord, Paris. 1987

18 Ricardo Muti conducts the orchestra at a rehearsal in The Mann Center for the Performing Arts, Philadelphia. 1988

19 Composer John Cage works with David Tudor at the Royal Festival Hall, London. 1972

a selection of well-known and unknown artists and musicians. The programming model assumes that the festival directors, globally acclaimed and respected in their fields, set up a relationship between the artists they respect and admire, and local audiences. While this model has many operational challenges, it is a useful early example of a programming initiative that attained a certain degree of popular culture star power as a means of introducing audiences to unknown artists. It was a cohesive and exciting new conception of how arts centres define themselves and engage with popular culture that heralded a new wave of curated music events around the globe, and gathered a momentum and international reputation much greater than the sum of its parts.

IN AUSTRALIA, FERGUS LINEHAN'S *ABOUT An Hour* series during his tenure as artistic director of the Sydney Festival from 2006 to 2009 exemplifies a programme that created a successful context for the presentation of new and risky work. These short works by international artists largely unknown to Sydney audiences were specifically promoted for their brevity and accessible ticket prices. The series was so successful it was co-opted by a federal government-funding agency as a means of introducing audiences to Australian choreographic talent. Some such programmes meet with instantly success and immediately connect with local communities; others can, of course, take some years to establish a reputation and a brand before flourishing.

LIKE MOST ARTS CENTRES, THE Sydney Opera House had tended in the past to produce annual or bi-annual programme series centred around a particular discipline (the theatre, world music) or a specific audience (kids, families, schools). This approach enabled the organisation to take advantage of the dynamic availability of its venues throughout the year, as well as of the changing tour schedules of international artists. While some such series have been successful and popular, particularly those programmes with a highly targeted niche market, others only began to succeed when high-profile names from the sphere of popular culture were tactically included in specific fields to help generate interest in the overall programmes.

WITNESSING CHANGE AND EXPERIMENTATION WITH programming approaches in arts centres worldwide and observing the explosion of contemporary music and literary festivals across the globe over the last decade, we clearly see that arts centres can seize the opportunity to present and position events in similar ways. Programming groups of shows under the banner of a short, focused festival-style event commands significantly higher levels of media and public attention, building cultural brands unique to organisations and often improving commercial results. An annual season of events rarely generates the same excitement as a festival-style launch in which a critical mass of activity engenders anticipation and interest greater than the sum of

20 Dancers from Merce Cunningham Dance Company performing during *Anniversary Events* tour under the Danish artist Olafur Eliasson's installation *The Weather Project* at Turbine Hall in Tate Modern, London. 2003

21 Scene of the opera *Man and Boy: Dada* by Michael Nayman at Almeida Theatre, London. 2004

its parts. Festivals, and hubs of activity around a governing theme, have grown in number and scope around Australia in the last ten years and consistently reveal the importance of this model as a means of marshalling the community's engagement with the arts. They have proven their capacity to connect with new audiences and in far greater numbers than those previously attending individual one-off events. There is also other untapped potential to support other organisational goals (such as maximising revenues from the private sector, for instance) through the creation of a series of new sponsorship properties, and exploiting opportunities afforded by participatory digital platforms.

THE SUCCESS OF THESE INITIATIVES lies in the fact that they do not decry the efforts of the many arts centres worldwide whose economic circumstances force them to turn to the opportunistic sharing of touring productions. Such initiatives usually emerge within overall strategies that expect maximum levels of venue utilisation alongside challenging commercial programming or hiring targets. While most arts organisations have to embrace commercial and subsidised events in their programming mix, these targets frequently dominate the way programmes are developed and, in my view, are not the means by which artists' work is best presented.

IF THE ARTISTIC LEADERS OF organisations have the economic freedom to establish the artistic framework for their decision-making, lead the development of new strategies and programming initiatives, and assume responsibility for more sophisticated artistic planning and event selection they are better able to offer cohesive and thoughtful programmes that develop audiences' knowledge and understanding of artists and the art forms they represent, their local and international exponents and the way they are influencing or being influenced by other forms. As long as their choices are informed by audience and peer feedback and are subject to ongoing artistic review, artistic heads can lead "taste development" among audiences consistently and rigorously. This approach to programming is more considered and is truly in the service of artists and the art forms they represent rather than an assortment of events that develop opportunistically as a result of commercial, touring or venue-hire opportunities.

THE CHALLENGES ARTS CENTRES FACE may change but they seldom decrease: aging equipment or inappropriate resources, challenging relationships with stakeholders and hirers, diminishing government financial support, complex community engagement ambitions that address the balance between commercial and subsidised activities and box-office risk, new audience demographics and the impact of digital technologies. All these issues and more play a part in the daily life of arts centre managers and their programming teams. The work is hard, complex, contradictory,

22 Rehearsal of the opera
Un Ballo in Maschera by
Giuseppe Verdi in Bregenzer
Festspiele, Bregenz. 2000

frustrating, often undervalued and frequently at arms-length from the arts it serves. So why do it? In the words of John Tusa, managing director of London's Barbican Arts Centre from 1995 to 2007:

> "The arts matter because they are local and relevant to the needs and wishes of local people. They help citizens to express their needs and to clothe them in memorable forms. They offer a way of expressing ideas and wishes that ordinary politics do not allow. The arts are immediate, intense and owned by the people who create them. The arts regenerate the rundown and rehabilitate the neglected. Arts buildings lift the spirits, create symbols that people can identify with, and give identity to places that may not have one. The arts teach the young to create, inspire the imagination and believe in their own potential. Where the arts start, jobs follow, jobs which are individualistic, independent and forward looking. Anywhere that neglects the arts, short changes its people."

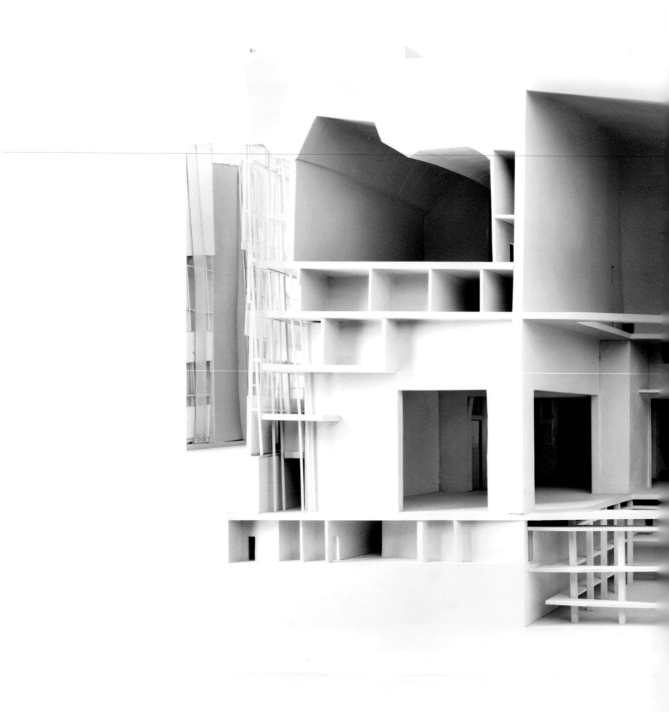

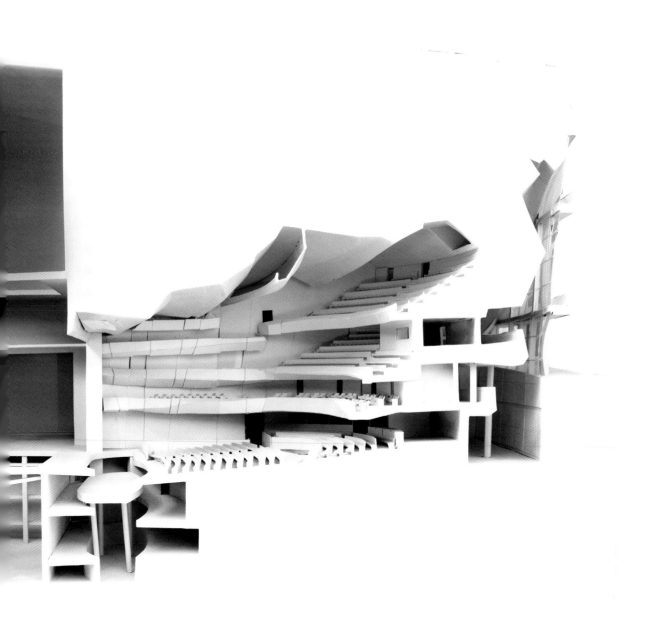

Cidade da Cultura de Galicia IX 2010

PETER BROOK

THREADS OF TIME

PETER BROOK

Threads of Time. A Memoir. London: Methuen Drama, 1998

[...]

Perhaps India is the last place where every period of history can still coexist, where the ugliness of neon lighting can illuminate ceremonies that have not changed in ritual form nor in outer clothing since the origin of the Hindu faith.

In Madurai, there is a huge temple, a sort of city where a single step takes one into another World. Time is not abolished—it does not seem to exist at all in these greate dark inner passages, where a dense mass of plump men, all naced but for a strip of twisted cloth round the waist, make eddies and whirls in a river of humanity. Light leads to darkness, darkness to shadowy limbs, to oil lamps. Sudden cries from voices fight with calls from long shinging horns; on walls striped alternately black and white, devotees hurl fistfuls of powder against pillars, streaking them red, or else rub colored earth on the trunks of carved elephants, caking the stone. Every child dreams of a time machine for exploring the past. It exists: an Indian temple is such a machine. Step into it and ancient Babylon is at your feet.

One night in Benares, a waving banner of lights came slowly out of the darkness, accompanied by the powerful trumpeting of musicians. As it approached, the lights took on the triple pattern of Shiva's emblem, in the form of a series of neon tubes strapped like tridents to the heads of naced men. It seemed to be a procession of penitent slaves linked together by long and dusty serpents, a strange bondage that finally revealed itself to be a fat cable leading to a bicycle, on which a figure in cotton trousers dripping with perspiration was forcing down the reluctant pedals to drive a rusty dynamo on wheels. The time machine brings you back to today.

A temple in India is a marketplace in no way separate from the street; it is a place for families and a noisy kitchen where priests rush from one boiling cauldron to another to store fires, stir liquids, or anoint sacrificial rocks with milk. There is no silence, only activity, as the gods feed indiscriminately on the energy of elephants, beggars, and Brahmans, all of whom bear the same sacred symbols streaked across face, body, or trunk in yellow paste; it is only on the steps that lead down to the vast tanks of slightly stagnant water that there is a slackening of the fever, for here the women slip into the cool wetness until their saris stick to their flash like patterned skin. The ground teems with insects and rats, and even the air is incessantly alive, with monkeys swinging along telegraph wires or hiding behind elaborately carved figures on the temple walls. There is no simplicity of form—how could there be?—for here the sacred art is a reflection of the secular life, and this life has no simplicity, only and inexhaustible variety that is always in movement.

Yet there is supreme, unattainable, ultimate deity of formless stillness, Brahma, who encompasses all movement and rules beyond the heavens, beyond God, beyond human understanding. The phenomenal universe demands a division into three: Brahma, Shiva, and Vishnu, whose form are complex and interchanging, and as they too are still unattainable to human understanding, they are compelled to subdivide again, so that only through an exact genealogy of intricate family relationships between great-aunt goddesses and third-cousin gods can we glimpse and explanation of the diversity of our daily experience.

Accordingly, a temple is not a static object to be contemplated; it is a journey to be undertaken, a store to be visited, a theology to be understood. Each carved figure, dancing, offering, and coupling, is like a word or sentece withing the syntax of a text. For a Brahman, the act of walking through one courtyard alter another to reach the sacred flame is like a passage thorugh pages of script; this is not far removed from the experience of the Australian Aborigine moving through his landscape, where the rocks and mounds are "songlines," the words of unwritten myths.

***

It had all begun with the young Indian who, during the rehearsals of our play about Vietnam, *US*, had first mentioned the strange word *Mahabharata* to me. The image he evoked had haunted my mind. Two great armies face one another, straining at the leash. In between them stands a prince, who asks, "Why must we fight?"

Again and again, I returned to this picture. Once day I told Jean-Claude Carrière about the battle, about the warrior's questions. He wanted to know more, and we went to call on Philippe Lavastine, the scholar friend who had dedicated his life to Sanskrit studies. We asked him to explain to us the situation of the two armies, and who was the prince and why does he question the meaning of war? Philippe began by telling us the name of the prince—Arjuna. Then he said that we needed to understand why his chariot was being driven by Krishna, a god. But to understand this, he continued, we needed to know all about Arjuna's brothers and his cousins, why they were in conflict and how they were born, and for this we had to go back to a long time before they were even conceived, to the creation of the world. Darkness fell, and when we left late in the evening, the tiny apartment crammed with books and papers seemed to glow with the great epic that was just beginning to unroll. The next day we returned. Now one breathless and amzing sessions followed another as the store continued, not in a logical order, but as Philippe remenbered it, in all its intricate criss-crossing complexity. Then, one night, the store was finished. We had received it as a child does in India, orally, from a storyteller. Leaving in silence, we found ourselves in the dark, deserted *rue* Saint André des Arts. We paused. We knew we shared the same decision. We could not keep what we had heard to ourselves. We had to pass it on to others throught our special field, the theater.

For ten years Jean-Claude read, wrote, and struggled. Version after version of the story came and went. Workshops with different groups of actors were started and left incomplete. It was as though the *Mahabharata*, which had lain asleep for so many centuries, suddenly awoke. It had needed to come out and cross the world. Luckily for us, we were there to help it on its way.

More and more journeys now became necessary and we returned to India many times over the years to prepare the *Mahabharata*. We—the word arises constantly, because for years "we" had become a changing, evolving team. "We" in India were sometimos Maurice Benichou and Alain Maratrat, two actors who had been with the French ensemble and had joined us to become part of *Timon of Athens*; they were to stay on, year after year, invaluable companions through many adventures and an indivisible part of the preparation of others. Alain loves all forms of movement; he is always close to the experience of his body and for the *Mahabharata* he plunged into learning all he could about the martial arts from tradition to tradition. Maurice had already placed the mysterious Hoopoe in *The Conference of the Birds*, which had oponed a whole new area in his sensibility, and now he was facing the dauting challenge of the role of Krishna.

There was also Jean-Claude Carrière, in the tenth year of his patient and sensitive search for the heart of the *Mahabharata*, never satisfied, always open to criticism, untiring, never short of ideas, writing all the time. He would read new scenes to us as they came off his pen in taxis, hotel rooms, and airport lounges where the planes were reliably late, living us plenty of time to work. For Jean-Claude, this was the climax not only of all we had done together but of his film scripts, his literary experiments, his wide reading, and his philosophical reflections. Suddenly, the *Mahabharata* was there to call on his thinking and bring together the wide range of his experiences. I cannot imagine a better collaborator. I know that without him the project could never have come into being.

Equally central to our work was Chloé Obolensky, proving again the inestimable value of the mutual understanding that comes from affection, respect, and trust, built on challenges lived through togheter. Chloé had joined us at the Bouffes to design *The Cherry Orchard*. Now she would listen to the readings and then vanish, indefatibably searching for objects and texturas in every bazaar.

Menawhile, watching and noting, serving as eye and ear for us all, was Marie-Hélène Estienne. Many years before, Micheline Rozan had first spoken of Marie-Hélène as a young person who she felt had very inusual talents, although she could not tell what from they would eventually take. When I met Marie-Hélène at dinner in Micheline's flat, my first impression was of a tense, silent figure refusing to be drawn into the chatter and the laughter. The next day we met again rapidly discovered we shared the same birthday—the first day of spring, though the years are far apart. Gradually a deep and close relationship came into being, and she entered into every facet of our work, until her talent and intuition became a vital part of each new experience. With lighting rapidity, she would plan our activities in precise detail; when we needed new actors, she would discover them in odd corners of the world through some astonishing and unpredictable precess of her own; when not working on texts, she would maintain the cast members' peace of mind with sorely tried affection and hardly concealed impatience. To this day, she changes her mind as often as I do, if not more, as the only way to reach a firm decision.

When we began to rehearse for the *Mahabharata*, we tried to share our impressions of India with the large group of actors, but we soon saw that this was imposible, so we scooped up our company and flew them to India. Jean-Claude, Marie-Héleène, and I had picked an itinerary in which every significant place we had visited over the years was now crammed together into ten days of breathless travel. This proved a very good method: a surfeit of indigestible impressions is part of the Indian experience and is a reminder that the conclusions one draws can never be complete; whenever one dreams that the outlines of India are beginning to become clear, a sudden new impression tips the previous structure on its head.

In the *Mahabharata*, the most commonly reapeated metaphor is that of a river. The battlefield is a river, the severed limbs are rocks, the amputated fingers are little fish, the torrent is blood. India is such a river. As soon as we arrived, we thrust the actors into the vast dark whirlpool of the great temple of Udipi, eating off palm leaves, squatting on the sotne floor like the hundreds of thousands of pilgrims who are fed there each year. We quickly found old Brahmans who were ready to talk about the *Mahabharata*, and after this first introduction, we lead the group to our favorite among all the holy spots we knew, a tiny temple called Parasinikadavu by a river deep in the Kerala countryside. Here the most ancient of rituals takes place, not at a special season but twice each day, and nowhere is the sense of ancientness more powerful. Within a small, crowded stone circle, enclosed in iron bars, six near-naked drummers pound on long drums, while in the flickering oil linght a small, brisa man caked in yellow paste, with ornate half-moon-shaped plates extending his lips, leaps and dances, aiming an arrow at each cardinal corner with a tiny silver bow. In this minuscule vault we felt in direct contact with the Vedic world in which the intricate actions of the *Mahabharata* had taken shape. The dichotomy between past and present was dissolved.

We journeyed with the actors in a cricle, down through Kerala, across Tamil Nadu, up to Madras, over to Calcutta, by train to Benares, then to Delhi, living each of us a store of vital images and the group as a whole an enourmous spool of impressions to be edited in rehearsal when we returned. At the same time, holding us firmly in reality was the India of today: swarming and limping, shoving and struggling in its misery, immobile in beggary, or huddled in sidewalk sleep. This washes the brain of any vestiges of romanticism, any lingering dreams of an East veiled in mystery. India was the night train, the stifling hot metal cylinder with tarnished metal bunks and barred windows through which thin hands would grope at each station for any match left carelessly under a pillow. It was godheads whose divinity is outlined with colored electric bulbs. It was the reality of starvation, the reality of violence, the reality of the irresistible cascade of life enveloping both shape and time.

Giddy and surfeited by the impressions we were receiving, about halfway through the journey, in Madurai, I felt we had to make a stop. We talked together at breakfast, and everyone agreed that we needed to rehearse. Our journey had a strict aim, and the pressing needs of the coming performance meant that our experiences needed to be related to our work. We left the city and walked to a nearby forest where, finding a clearing, we gave ourselves as the beginning of an exercise the task of selecting one natural object from among the trees and collecting them at the clearing's edge. We had hardly finished doing so when, as if out of nowhere, an old lady appeared and quietly postrated herself before our homemade pile. After a while she rose, stepped backward, and was gone, leaving us to recognize with astonishment that we had added one more to India's shrines.

I them proposed another exercise: "Very rapidly, going round the circle, let each person produce one word, one word only, to pinpoint his most vivid impressions of India." There was no hesitation; like a swift percussion, beat upon beat, adjective or noum followed like the many facets of a rotating cristal: "frenzy," "color," "tranquility," "age," "vulgarity," "hunger," "faith," "splendor," "misery," "matriarchy" —thirty people, thirty different words that seemed so inadequate that at once we made another round, thirty more words after which we left off, accepting that the list could never be complete. It now seemed an interesting moment to rehearse one of the scenes we had evolved in the Bouffes du Nord, to see what the influences of the journey could bring to it. We had hardly begun when we saw that the forest was full of hidden human life. An audience had assembled and was watchning us intently through the leaves. "What can they make of all this?" I wondered as Jean-Claude's French text enrolled. An actor sprang out from the bushes. "Shiva!" came an immediate cry of recognition from our very first spectators. We were overwhelmed. Our sounds and gestures made sense in India. This, more than anything else, gave us the courage to pursue what up to then had been completely untested work.

Near Madras there is a holy place. Kanchipuram, a sacred center, a city of temles. It is one of the tour great shrines making a square across the subcontinent that are devoted to the tradition of Shankaracharya, a fourth-century saint and teacher. Here, in the busy cluster of buildings in his name, there are three Shankaracharyas. There is an old master, who has withdrawn from the world; he no longer speaks, but he can be seen from the courtyard once or twice a day, in silence, venid a face-sized shutter that ismomentarily opened and closed. There is also another occasion when the people who wish to participate in his charismatic aura gather on a balcony, on seats, and wait patiently as in a theater in from of a curtain. Sometimes it is never drawn back. But if they are fortunate, it will part without warning. Then, on a lightly coger level to the terrace, lying on the floor in a narrow cubicle can be seen a motionless huddle, for which no words are more apt than the phrase in the *Bhagavad-Gita*, "Time grown old." If the ancient figure can be persuaded to rise, the croad presses forward, and some may even be allowed to come down a few steps as far as an iron mailing. The old man's eyes will now scan the expectant faces, and if this glance is met even for an instant, the observer receives the moment of contact physically, like a shock.

There is a second Shakaracharya, in the thick of life, who has all the energy necessary to serve a leader's practical obligations and is reponsible for the running of the temple. Once day, the old man will die, and then the second Shankaracharya will take the old man's place behind the shutter, while the third Shankaracharya, now still a young boy being rigorously prepared by daily ruties, will step into the second position, and a new boy will be chosen to enter the chain.

The active Shankaracharya, a quick-faced man always ready to switch from laughter to seriousness, eyes alert and dark, stripes of paste on his forehead, a chest bare but for the Brahman's diagonal ritual thread, a staff in his hand, welcomed us warmly. On a previous visit, I had asked him a question about Krishna. Krishna is god incarnate; he descended to live as man, taking on the suffering of humanity, but unlike Christ he also took on man's activities and pleasures: in the old stories he was a tremendous and cunning warrior and an irresistible lover with twenty thousand wives. He thus reflects the generous Hindu capacity to encompass every aspect of living experience without moral judgment. Does this make him perfect or imperfect? Is impefection beyond perfection? "If Krishna has all the aspects of a man," I asked, "has he therefore man's natural ability to be wrong, to make errors?" I truly needed to hear his answer, hoping perhaps to find my own weaknesses condoned or at least to understand better the *Mahabharata*. Shakaracharya smiled. "You put this question from a man's point of view," he answered. "A man's mind is torced to make such distinctions. From Krishna's point of view, the question cannot arise." Like a Zen riddle, these words shocked my understanding and showed how much more is revealed by the way of bafflement that by the deceptive ways of reason.

This time Shakarachrya welcomed tose of us who had been there before as old friends. We sat on the ground, and I explained that we had brought with us the group of actors who were working on the play. He pointed to them one by one and lughingly identified the characters. Elsewhere, India had often been racist, and repellent questions would be put again and again such as "Why a black man?" "Why black?" Here there was no barrier; to our delight and relief he immediately saw a Hindu hero or deity—a Bhishma, a Drona, a Shiva, or a Krishna—in the African, Japanese, Balinese, or French face turned expectantly toward him. He blessed our undertaking, advised us not to eat meta on the day of the first performance, and asked if we could send him a videotape when the play was ready.

For once, this was a travler's promise that would not be forgotten, and when five years later we made a film of the play we sent him a copy. Shortly after that, some of us returned to India. As we entered Kanchipuram a croad of young people collected excitedly, recognizing the actors. "We saw the film!" "Where?" "At the temple." "Very nice movie!" We visited Shankaracharya, who was as active, humorous, and practical as before, and he told us he approved of our version. He was for us our ultimate critic, whom we both trusted and feared.

The more we entered into the *Mahabharata*, the more we came to recognize the richness and generosity of the original Hindu thought. One single untraslatable word, *dharma*, is sufficient to link the universal with the uniquely personal. The cosmos has its Dharma, and each individual has his or her own dharma; our obligation is to discover this, understand it, and make its realization our constant aim. The word is often feebly translated as "duty;" in fact, if implies living in accordance with an imperative that goes beyond all simple moral laws. Dharma respects each person's inborn limits, so each has his or her own starting point, and within the span of one life each man or woman can only go just so far. We each have our destiny, but few of us actually allow our destiny to appear. Dharma cannot be reduced to any code, but it can be reawakened in the puzzled seeker by the whole mythic action of the *Mahabharata*, which shows how an individual's dharma is related to the great Dharma, to the constant rebalancing of the scales of existence. In the *Mahabharata*, Krishna shows that to preserve the balance of the universe, everything must have its place. Sexuality, duplicity, violence—each has a meaning. Thus his unexpected and apparently inmoral actions are a constant confrontation with rigid thinking and can even shock true Hindu believers. At a social gathering in Delhi, a distinguished lady burst into tears. "I can't bear the Krishna of the *Mahabharata*," she said to me. "He behaves so badly."

Such misinterpretations are part of the all-embracing nature of the *Mahabharata*, and in our rehearsals we were continually provoked by the contradictions that are part of this work. We often called it Shakespearean, because every schematic idea is blown open by the true humanity of the characters. This sets them beyond easy moralizing and facile judgments.

The journey with the actors to India was perhaps the most important part of our rehearsal process, not so much as a way of putting everyone "in the mood" but as a way of eliminating *clichés* about the East and about myths in general. Every moment brought a new surprise, a new contradiction, and although we traveled light, we returned to Paris with an excess of intellectual and emotional baggage.

Now the practical task was to find theatrical forms that would be suitable carriers for this load. More than ever in our work, it was clear that forms had to come last, that the true character of the performance would only emerge when a hodgepodge of styles had passed through a filter to eliminate the superfluous. Our only principle was first to discover meaning for ourselves, then find the action that makes it meaningful to others. So in this process nothing could be refused, everything had to be explored. We imitated ancient techniques, knowing that we would never be able to do them well. We fought, chanted, improvised, told stories, or we introduced fragments from each of the group's widely different traditions. The path passed through chaos and muddle toward order and coherent. But time worked for us. Suddenly the day came when the whole group found that it was telling the same store. The different races, the different traditions working together had become a single mirror for a multiplicity of themes.

A century ago the vision of history that ancient Hinduism proposed was quite unacceptable to the West, but its imagery and symbols are becoming more and more confirmed in the present-day world. The Hindu relieves that, in the endless cycles of creation and annhibilation, human beings rapidly reached the Golden Age, the first and highest Yuga from which the subsequet ones descend. The lowest, the fourth and last period, is the one in which we live today: Kali Yuga, the Black Age. This is not pessimism; reality can be neither optimistic nor pessimistic, it is as it is, and this is exactly why this myth is so relevant. All the stress and anguish, the violent misery and despair of contemporary life are reflected in the complex events of the great epic. Our world is sliding deeper and deeper into the bitter abominations that the *Mahabharata* predicted; the age of darkness is all around us, and with it we seem to reach the ultimate degradation of the human creature—far beyond all that the ancient authors could foresee.

Today, we have many astonishing films, plays, and novels on the horrors of war, but unlike them, the *Mahabharata* is not negative. It leads one into the basic meaning of conflict. It shows that the movements of history are inevitable, that great miseries and disasters may be unavoidable, but within each passing moment a new possibility can open, and life can still be lived in all its fullness. This can help us understand how to live. It can help us cross the darkest age. This alone was reason enough for staging the work. This is why, in French, then in English, touring across the world, and then on tape and on film, it seems to have touched a common human chord. How to survive is an urgent contemporary question, but it can easily cover up a far greater question, which the *Mahabharata* places firmly in its rightful place —not only how to survive, but why?

[…]

Galicia— A Culture Between Europe and America

Ramón Villares

Starting from its original French root, the word "promenade" *is linked to the idea of a stroll that usually takes place in a public park or a tree-lined avenue, on a road that runs along the bank of a river or the seashore, or in any* locus amoenus *we may imagine and where, as well as enjoying the contact with nature, strollers converse peripatetically. It also acts as a powerful metaphor to express one of the most common passions in human nature—the desire to avoid the routine tiredness of everyday life or fulfil our curiosity regarding the unknown. In any event, it is important to combine the action of moving and strolling with the exchange of ideas through pleasant conversation or the discovery of new spaces and places. We could, however, start from the idea of the* promenade *as a comprehensive metaphor of the past reality of a country and a culture and as an invitation to imagine its future. On this occasion, we propose a stroll through Galicia, its history, its culture and what used to be called its* soul *and now tends to be referred to as identity. A stroll conceived from the inside but with the help of the outer gaze; the gaze of travellers when they describe their impressions of what they have seen in Galicia, but also the stereotyped gaze that has been configured as a synthesis of Galicia at the heart of an externally shaped imaginary.*

1 Cathedral of Santiago
de Compostela [*Le Monde
Illustre*, n. 1220, detail].
14th of August of 1880

STARTING FROM ITS ORIGINAL FRENCH root, the word "*promenade*" is linked to the idea of a
stroll that usually takes place in a public park or a tree-lined avenue, on a road that runs along
the bank of a river or the seashore, or in any *locus amoenus* we may imagine and where, as well
as enjoying the contact with nature, strollers converse peripatetically. It also acts as a powerful
metaphor to express one of the most common passions in human nature—the desire to
avoid the routine tiredness of everyday life or fulfil our curiosity regarding the unknown.
In any event, it is important to combine the action of moving and strolling with the exchange
of ideas through pleasant conversation or the discovery of new spaces and places. Ours are
not favourable times for these social practices, and neither are the urban parks and the
paths around cities and villages able to welcome the presence of strollers every day unless
they become jogging heroes. We could, however, start from the idea of the *promenade* as
a comprehensive metaphor of the past reality of a country and a culture and as an invitation
to imagine its future. On this occasion, we propose a stroll through Galicia, its history, its
culture and what used to be called its *soul* and now tends to be referred to as identity.

A STROLL CONCEIVED FROM THE inside but with the help of the outer gaze; the gaze of
travellers when they describe their impressions of what they have seen in Galicia, but also
the stereotyped gaze that has been configured as a synthesis of Galicia at the heart of an
externally shaped imaginary. The culture and the idea of Galicia can be approached in many
ways. In this case it is the idea of the stroll that should mark the main line of interpretation,
so that what will stand out are the movement and the path, the comings and goings.
I shall start by what is most obvious, the spatial situation of Galicia and the configuration
of its territory with real boundaries, and then proceed to observe the key concepts of this
promenade: the fact being a point of arrival or a way in but also a way out for travellers
to "overseas" harbours, pilgrims on their way back home and thousands of emigrants
who took transoceanic routes to the American *El Dorado*. Finally, I shall draw attention to
Galicia as the cradle of a culture and a language that for a variety of historical circumstances
can be regarded a distinctive and unique view of the world and a bridge between the two
powerful and widespread Iberian cultures of Spanish and Portuguese origin.

I   From *callaici* to Galician and Portuguese

THE CONFIGURATION OF PRESENT-DAY Galicia is the result of a historical process with
mediaeval roots that began with the formation of the kingdom of Portugal. In the case of
Galicia, the identification between a cultural and political reality and a specific territorial
space was historically precocious. It is barely possible to come across an older example of

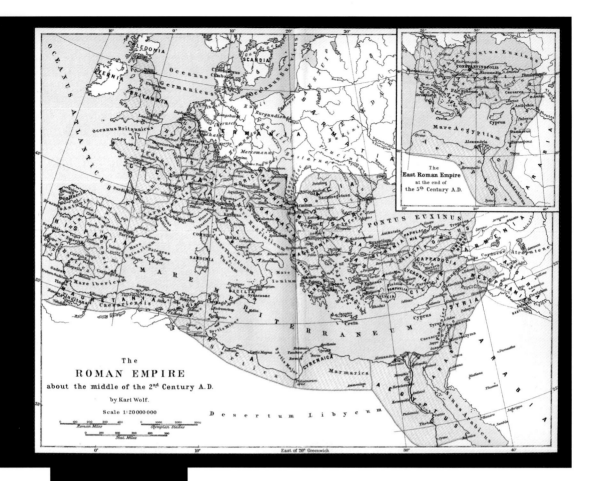

2 Map of the Roman Empire about the middle of the 2nd century. [*The World's History. The Mediterranean Nations*, William Heineman: vol. IV n. 1220]. Dr. H. F. Helmolt, 1902

the definite establishment of political and cultural frontiers, or of the identification between history and territory anywhere in Europe. The territory of the Kingdom of Galicia had been established at its present boundaries in the early twelfth century, with the exception of the episcopal districts (Astorga, Tui, Oviedo) that remind us how deep-seated the ecclesiastical organisation of the territory is in comparison with its lay administration.

NEITHER THE ECCLESIASTIC OR LAY elites of *Gallaecia* in the late eleventh century and first decades of the twelfth century were responsible for this early establishment of the Galician frontiers. On the contrary, we could say that it was based on several decisive facts, one of which was the actual identification, since Roman times, of the most western parts of Iberia with the tribe of the *callaici*, that provided the name for the entire western province of Roman Hispania. Although the frontiers of this Roman *Gallaecia* were vague, the territory extended south to the Mondego and east to the river basin of the Duero plateau. The place name *Gallaecia*, however, prevailed over the three Roman convents and the territory thus acquired a formal unity that derived from a certain social and cultural homogeneity. The fact that a soldier of Galician origin called Rufino, who had died in the province of Tarraco at the end of the second century AD was buried under an inscription that defined him as *callaecus*, proves the identity force of its origin. Similarly, the fact that Baquiario, a disciple of Prisciliano's, should have been considered more suspect of heterodoxy on account of the region he came from than the ideas he professed, substantiates the importance of the land in the shaping of identity.

HOWEVER, THE TERRITORIAL DIMENSION OF Roman *Gallaecia*, which with a few changes was moved to the kingdom of the Swabians and subsequently to the kingdom of Galicia in the early Middle Ages, would be definitely established between the last years of the eleventh century and the first decades of the twelfth century. Aymeric Picaud, author of the well known *Codex Calixtinus*, clearly warns that "past the land of León and the passes on Mount Irago and Mount Cebreiro, is the land of the Galicians." For a twelfth-century traveller on the French Road the mountains of León already appeared as an eastern *limes* of Galicia, at least from an ethnic and cultural point of view, for among all the peoples the Road crosses, Galicians are considered to be the most similar to the inhabitants of Gaul or Franks. This was the time when the southern boundaries, of greater political transcendence, were also defined.

THE CRUCIAL PERIOD FROM THE late eleventh century to the first half of the twelfth century witnessed several decisive facts for the history of Galicia and Portugal. In the first place, the Don García's reign as king of Galicia once the kingdom had been divided up by his father Ferdinand I, who had died in 1065. The existence of a king of Galicia was a novelty after centuries in which the so-called Astur-Leonese kingdom had overshadowed the true kingdom of western Christians, the kingdom of Galicia, as recognised by Merovingians, Muslims and even Popes. However, the brief reign of king Don García (1065–1071)

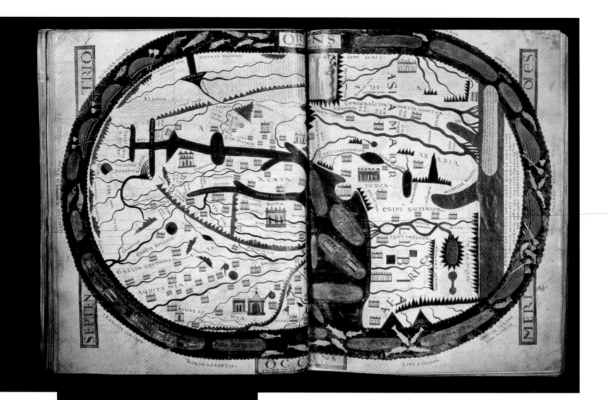

3 World Map from "The Apocalypse of Saint John" [*Manuscrito de Saint-Sever*: MS LATIN 8878 ff. 45bisv–45ter]. Beatus of Saint-Sever, *c.* 1060

prevented the consolidation of a dynasty in the territory known as the kingdom of Galicia which, in the opinion of Murguía, was the "most favourable occasion for founding the Galician monarchy [*A ocasión máis propicia de fundar a monarquía galega*]." In territorial terms it was a broad empire that embraced the legacy of the Swabian monarchy and extended from the Ortegal to south of the Duero. Subsequent events, such as the division of Galicia into two countships attributed to Burgundian counts married to Urraca (Raymond) and Teresa (Henry), made way for the definite establishment of the inner borders of Don García's kingdom.

ANOTHER SIGNIFICANT FACT WAS THE formation of the kingdom of Portugal starting from the territory of Braga ruled by count Henry and his son Alfonso Henriques, in which the figures of Archbishop Diego Gelmírez and the Leonese monarch Alfonso VI also played a transcendental role. This was a time of great changes in the affairs of state of the mainland and Galicia appeared as a political epicentre. As a result of the birth of the Portuguese kingdom (that "inexplicable and unexplained event," according to Claudio Sánchez-Albornoz) and the move of the Galician nobility (led by Fernando Peres de Trava) to the Leonese and Portuguese courts, the kingdom of Galicia was reduced to its present territorial limits—in other words, to the old convent of Lugo with a few extra areas taken from those of Braga (south of the province of Ourense) and Asturias (Valdeorras and adjoining regions). This was the greatest division of Roman *Gallaecia*, which Romantic historian Benito Vicetto described as one of the most important landmarks in the history of Galicia. In his study *Mitteleuropa* (1934), Vicente Risco evoked his trip to Germany in 1930 to become a boarding student. In Hendaya, a line of Portuguese emigrants prompted him to write, "While Lugo surrendered unarmed and forgotten, Braga managed to extend Galicia to the Algarve, preserve her independence and create new Galicias in America, Africa, India, China and Malaysia. While the history of the Galicia of Lugo was a constant political failure, Portuguese Galicia represented the victory of the ideal Galicia, Galician Galicia [*Namentres a Galicia lucense se entregou inerme e esquecida, os bracarenses souberon alongar Galicia deica o Algarve, sostela independente, e crear novas Galicias na América, na África, na India, na China e na Malasia. Namentres a historia da Galicia lucense é un perpetuo fracaso político, a de Portugal representa o triunfo da Galicia ideal, da Galicia galega*]."

THIS SWIFT TERRITORIAL DEMARCATION OF the kingdom of Galicia was formalised by the existence of clearly established frontiers, but above all by the fact that they would remain unchangeable in the future. Indeed, for several centuries the political border with the kingdom of Portugal was so faint that it favoured a great degree of social and institutional permeability between the two banks of the Miño or of the dry line. The domains of the diocese of Tui extended over a number of regions on the left bank of the Miño and several descendants of the Galician nobility found shelter by marrying into noble Portuguese houses,

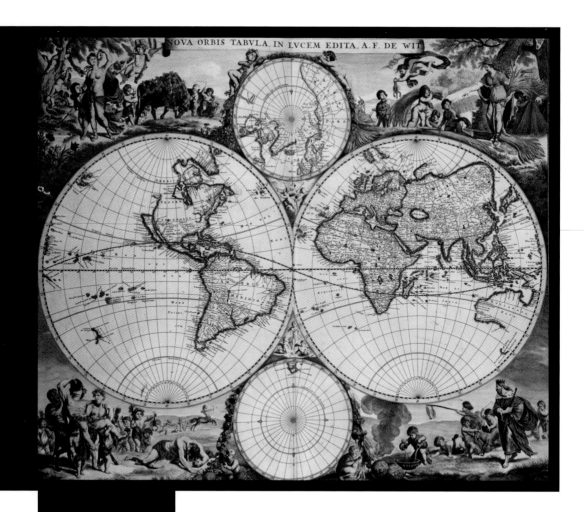

4 *Nova Orbis Tabvla, In Lucem Edita.* Frederick de Wit, 1662

as exemplified by Inés de Castro wedding count Fernández de Andeiro. From a political point of view, however, from the beginning of the twelfth century the kingdom of Galicia was prevented from extending southwards and furthermore occupied an eccentric position as regards the other western Christian kingdoms, those of Castilla y León. The joint policies of the Leonese monarchs against king Don García, of Gelmírez against the see in Braga and of Alfonso Enríquez in defence of the inhabitants of the Portuguese county prompted the transformation of the kingdom of Galicia into an end land, prevented from having a border or territorial *mark* that would have stabilised the different mediaeval Christian kingdoms. In other words, Galicia was deprived of one of the sources of history, i.e., making war.

THIS DIVISION OF FORMER *GALLAECIA* would have crucial consequences for the history of Galicia, although awareness of these consequences is the result of very modern intellectual thought. Borders, which in mediaeval times were still generous, would become increasingly rigid following the rule of the monarchy of the Philips over the Portuguese empire. The restoration of the Braganza dynasty in the Portuguese crown after 1640 was sharply disputed by the Galician nobility and aristocracy, even by military detachments, who fought against the Portuguese on the dry line and on the banks of the River Miño where a network of military fortresses was set up in the French Vauban style, proving the will to establish a political and military border on a cultural and linguistic *continuum* that had barely been questioned since mediaeval times. Portugal remained close by, on the other side of the River Miño, but its boundaries became increasingly impassable. Not until the appearance of nineteenth-century Iberian trends and, from the Galician point of view, the birth of political nationalism (from Murguía to Castelao, in particular) would Portugal begin to be seen as a key to the legitimisation of a federal Iberian political option that could contribute to the "re-Galicianisation" of Galicia.

II A *finis terrae* with an Apostle

AS WELL AS HAVING EXTREMELY old boundaries, another very obvious feature of Galicia is that it is the most western *finis terrae* or land's end on the European continent. This location, on the farthest corner of old Europe, may not be a merit of the inhabitants of the land but it clearly determines their ways and attitudes and above all how they are perceived from without. Iberian Galicia is one of the many land's ends that exist in the world, but it is the only case in which a bordering location has become a distinguishing feature, charged with cultural significance and profound meaning. The fact of being *finis terrae* implied, to quote Otero Pedrayo, transforming the *mare tenebrosum* of the oceanic sea into a "territorial mark," i.e., a border.

5 Map of northwest Spain.
19th century

THE REALITY OF BEING A European land's end had important consequences in Galicia's shaping of a national culture. The first of these was more a result of the slow pace of human and cultural diversity in Galicia than of its remoteness. One of the most precise elements in the forming of a culture is actually the existence of demographic mixes and confrontations between different alternatives (even via warfare). The patriarch Murguía already bemoaned this situation in his preliminary discourse to *Historia de Galicia* (1865–1866),[1] where he compared the advantage of Galicia being "A complete nationality [*Unha completa nacionalidade*]" to the fact that, separated by the vast plains of Castilla, "no other nation is knocking at its door [*ningunha outra nación chama ás súas portas*]."

MURGUÍA'S ASSERTION MAY BE UNDERSTOOD politically but in ethnic terms it is clearly biased. The arrival in Galicia of hordes of people from outside the region has been a constant since prehistoric times, as proven by successive waves of Celts. Later on, and in spite of their low numbers (some 30,000 individuals), the arrival of Swabians in the fifth century conditioned the territorial organisation and the cultural life of the Swabian reign for two centuries. Less representatively, other peoples of different ethnic origins would arrive in Galicia, ranging from the Castilians and Genoese of the Middle Ages to the hordes of Catalans of modern times, promoters of the salting industry, the Camerans (from the Cameros mountains) and the French Basques of the nineteenth century, pioneers of the textile trade and the tanning industry. While Galicia can be defined as a country of emigrants, as we shall see, it has never lost its ability to attract and welcome immigrants who would noticeably modify the human landscape of this Iberian land's end.

OTERO PEDRAYO STATED THAT GALICIA is the "west of the land of the Romans," but Vicente Risco also considered it the "south of the land of the Celts." Among the different Celtic nations of Atlantic Europe, Galicia occupied the most southern position in an imaginary Celtic land, which would also comprise Brittany, Ireland and Scotland. This position would have invited Galicia to take control of the oceanic sea. According to ancient texts and a long-standing literary tradition, the relations between the Galicia of megalithic times and the other *finis terrae* of the Atlantic would have been intense and frequent. Although these relations are not well documented, there are obvious cultural analogies between Atlantic peoples. However, it is not known whether these derive from the fact of belonging to the same Celtic ethnic group or from the frequency of their relations.

WEST OF THE LAND OF the Romans and south of the land of the Celts are two cultural definitions of Galicia that reflect its eccentric geographic position, an eccentricity that did not, however, entail either isolation or reclusiveness. Whether by land or by sea,

---

1   M. Murguía, *Historia de Galicia*, 2 vol. (Lugo: Imprenta de Soto Freire, 1965–1966).

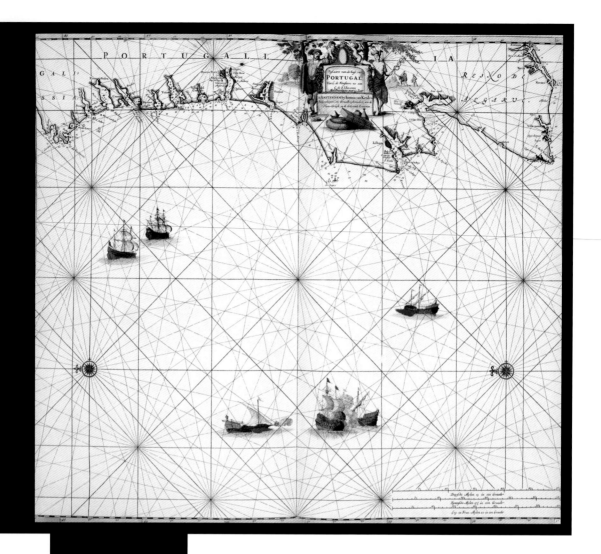

6 *Map of the Atlantic coast of Portugal.* Johannes van Kuelen, 1682

Galicia's relations with other countries were intense, especially after the ninth century, when Carolingian Europe found in the Milky Way a good reason for conquering a *finis terrae* called into question by the cultural and political splendour of Al-Andalus, located on the border of Christian Europe. That's when the sarcophagus of the apostle Santiago was *conceived*, in an almost unknown place (*in finibus Amaea*), by the bishop of Iria, Teodomiro. The discovery, immediately appropriated by the Christian monarchs in the kingdom of Galicia and Asturias, suddenly changed Galicia's position as a *finis terrae* and transformed this fact into the "Essential theme of the history of Galicia [*Tema esencial da historia de Galicia*]" in its relationship with universal history (Otero Pedrayo). Galicia thereby strengthened its status as a European culture at a time when the belief that the body of the apostle Santiago had been buried in Compostela attracted rumours from beyond the mountain passes disseminated by pilgrims travelling from the Île-de-France and Cluniac Burgundy, Roman Latium and the lands of the vast "Mitteleuropa" ruled by the Sacred Empire.

THE PILGRIMAGE TO SANTIAGO DE Compostela would have huge cultural, political and even geopolitical consequences as a result of its significance in the configuration of the mediaeval world under the central power of the city of Rome. It could also be understood as the construction of a "pacific alternative" to Jerusalem, as Juan Goytisolo has observed, in the historical context of European expansion towards the Mediterranean through the Crusades. But mention should also be made of some of the reasons for which this farthest corner of Roman territory became a place of reference for European culture. As Américo Castro noted, two of these reasons were very powerful. The first is the actual influence of the religiousness of the inhabitants of the former Roman *Gallaecia*, exemplified by deeply rooted rigorous movements such as Priscillianism, which had been contested since the fourth century although never totally eradicated. The cult of the apostle Santiago could have acted as an antidote to this legacy from late Roman times. The second is the intensity of so-called pagan rites in the sixth century, to judge by Martín de Dumio's *De correctione rusticorum*, a text that denounces many of the practices that had survived until recent times, such as lighting candles at crossroads, casting spells and enchantments, etc. Apart from these endogenous religious reasons, Islam and the Arab presence in the Iberian peninsula from the eighth century onwards were powerful challenges. Although Galicia remained outside of the sphere of Islamic influence, the transformation of the apostle Santiago into a religious and military referent (as suggested by the image of Saint James "The Moor-slayer") before the Islamic world strengthened the role of the basilica and of the city of Compostela, not just as a western counterweight in the geopolitical balance of the Christian world based in Rome but also as an alternative to the Cordoba of the Omeyas.

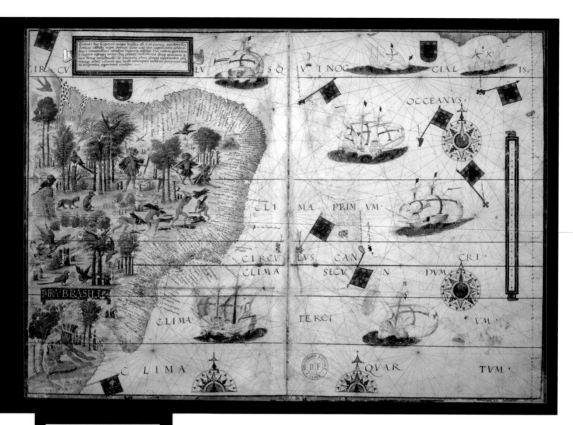

7 Hydrographic map of
Brazil [*Atlas Nautique
Portugais dit "Atlas Miller"*:
CPL GE DD 683 RES f. 5].
Loppo Homem, 1519

THE EMBLEMATIC FIGURE OF THE apostle Santiago combined his condition as a pilgrim, who attends universally to whoever approaches his sanctuary, with that of a knight fighting, as was his exclusive right, against the Moors, considered enemies or infidels in religious terms. His *conception* and subsequent transformation into a "Mecca" attracting pilgrims from the Christian world were the keystones of the position of the "small" Galicia—now separated from the Portuguese kingdom—in the geopolitical context of Christian Europe, and of its definition in religious and cultural terms. The tradition of the pilgrimage to Santiago de Compostela and the Way of Saint James in itself were essential factors in the shaping of Galicia as a *culture* and a *nation*, and at the same time served as political legitimisation of the so-called "Reconquest" and of the southward expansion of Christian kingdoms. In Castilla and Portugal the military Order of Santiago became one of the most politically active institutions in the defence of the border with Islam. In the words of scholar Bernardo Barreiro de Vázquez Varela, written on occasion of the discovery of the apostle's ashes in the crypt in Compostela in 1880, "the cornerstone of the cradle of the Spanish nation." One of the most powerful political allegories written in modern Spain, *El buho gallego*, attributed to the seventh Count Lemos, insisted precisely on this duplicity: the kingdom of Galicia should be respected in the "republic of the birds" for being the land where an apostle is buried and the birthplace of the Spanish monarchy of the House of the Hapsburgs.

THESE OLD CONTRADICTIONS HANGING OVER the son of Zebedee resurface today, when his figure is simultaneously celebrated (in adjoining places) on the Day of the Galician Homeland, a festivity introduced by the *Irmandades da Fala* nationalists, and at the (also patriotic) presentation of the King's Offering to the patron saint of Spain, Santiago, established by King Philip IV. The scholar Américo Castro noticed this contradiction upon arriving in Compostela for the first time returning from his American exile in 1957. About to start proof-reading his book *Santiago de España*, published in Buenos Aires in 1958, he confessed "[N]ever have I seen such a profusion of royal coats of arms as in Santiago." His impression is easily confirmed by the façades and altarpieces of the main monuments in the city, from the Obradoiro to Saint Martin Pinario and the School of Saint Jerome. But Américo Castro goes on to add that the coats of arms, *façades* and stones of the city reflect the universal and even imperial dimension of Santiago: "[T]he Apostle's basilica, the Obradoiro Square and the accompanying buildings were the expression of an imperial drive—of the empire of belief—which was initiated by the determined step of the Apostle's steed and would be continued in sixteenth-century enterprises, the construction of the Alcázar in Toledo, the huge reliquary at El Escorial, the Square of Arms in the city of Mexico (that rhymes in assonance with that of the Obradoiro), in the beauties of the Yucatecan Mérida…"

8 Alfonso VI [*Tumbo A*: CF 34, f. 26v, detail]. 1129–1134

9 Doña Urraca [*Tumbo A*: CF 34 f. 30r, detail]. 1129–1134

10 Fernando I [*Tumbo A*: CF 34 f. 26r, detail]. 1129–1134

III Echoes from Regions Beyond the Mountain Passes— A Return Journey

GALICIA WAS THE AREA BORDERING on European Roman lands, and the decline of the empire was a decisive incentive for this land to become a place of pilgrimage. According to an old Graeco-Jewish tradition, to march towards the West was the fate of all ancient empires, and Galicia became a gateway for numerous groups of people who arrived and settled there. Despite being a final destination, the journey was not unidirectional —those who made it to Galicia also returned to their homelands, and while they possibly brought "echoes from regions beyond the mountain passes" they also offered opportunities for making the journey back. From ancient times the fact of reaching Galician territory implied crossing several natural barriers, i.e., the eastern mountain passes of León and Cebreiro, as we learn in the *Codex Calixtinus*, the first guide book. But the pilgrims' way also encouraged the search for new borders beyond the passes of Galicia and the Pyrenees. The most pristine element in Galician culture is not, therefore, a delayed swing of forces rooted in a land's end but the result of a continuous mixture of that specific land's end (which is not always a periphery) and continental and Mediterranean space (which is not always a centre). Both the fact of being a gateway and the constant relationship with regions beyond the mountain passes—a fundamental component of both endogenous and exogenous ideas of Galicia—were privileged by the tradition of the religious journey to Santiago de Compostela and the development of a great road of pilgrimage of continental dimensions.

AYMERIC PICAUD'S DESCRIPTIONS IN THE *Codex Calixtinus* of the peoples a pilgrim could meet on the way from France to Compostela established quite notable differences between Gascons, Basques and Navarrese, whose forms of behaviour he felt were not befitting the cultural standards of Christian Europe. However, when it came to describing the Galician land and peoples he made an interesting observation: in spite of being litigant and bad-tempered, among all the peoples of Spain Galicians have more in common with the inhabitants of France, i.e., the Franks or the Gauls. This positive assessment reveals the existence of a cultural brotherhood between the Galicia of the Iberian *finis terrae* and the Galician lands over the passes of the Pyrenees, a brotherhood forged in Carolingian times by the long hand of Charlemagne and the fabrication of the apostle's sarcophagus. Over the course of time the presence of friars educated in the learned abbey of Cluny in eleventh-century Galicia, supported by the Castilian monarch Alfonso VI, proved that the influences from both sides of the Pyrenees had not been in vain. Indeed, the author of the *Codex Calixtinus* emphasised the poverty of the cities of the Way of Saint James in Spanish territories as opposed to the wealth of Compostela.

INCIPIT LIBER .VI. SCI. JACOBI. Apli.

ARGVMENTV(m) BEATI CALIXTI PP.

Si ueritas apuo lectore ni(r)s uoluminib; req̄ raf.
in huı codıcıs serie. amputato esitacionıs scru
pulo secure ıntelligat; Que enı ın eo scribū
tur. multı ad huc uıuentes uera ē̄ restantur;

Cap.ı.

VATVOR vıe sunt que ad
scm ıacobū tendentes ın unū ad
ponte regıne. ın horıs yspanıe co
adunantur; Alıa per scm eaıdıu.
& monte pessulanū. & tholosam. &
portus aspı tendıt. alıa p scam ma
rıam podıı. ꞇ scm fıdeon co quıs. et
scm petrū de moyssaco ıncedıt. alıa
p scam marıā magda
lenā vızılıacı. ꞇ scm
leonardū lemouıcensem. & urbe petragorıcensem pꞇꞇ.
alıa p scm martınū turonense. ꞇ scm ylarıs pıctauen
sem. & scm ıohem anglıacensem. & scm eutropıū sco
nensem. & urbe burdegalensem uadıt; Illa que p scam

12

11 Book V [*Liber Sancti
Jacobi, Codex Calixtinus*: CF
14, f. 192r]. C. 1137–1140

12 Apostle Saint James
[*La Legende Doree*: MS Royal
19 B XVII f. 176v, detail].
Jehan de Vignay, 1382

PARALLEL TO THE ESTABLISHMENT OF Galicia's territorial borders, the Way of Saint James opened up a great road linking ideas, people and goods, a road that connected the city of Compostela and its spatial surroundings with trans-Pyrenean and even transalpine culture, as explained by the terms "*transpirenavit*" and "*transalpinavit*" used to describe bishop Diego Gelmírez's trip to Rome in *Historia Compostellana*. But let's get back to Aymeric Picaud, for his remark is by no means innocent, and in fact reveals how much the Galician *finis terrae* owes to the power of Gaul, which would have left its own cultural mark on the land, one at least as significant as the territorial mark of the Catalan region, the Hispanic Mark. It also enables us to assess the importance of the tradition of the pilgrimage to Santiago de Compostela in the first centuries of the second millennium in the career of pope Calixto III: "[B]etween the eleventh and thirteenth centuries the whole of cultural Europe was in touch with Santiago [*Entre os séculos XI e XII, toda a Europa cultural está en contacto con Santiago*]," observed Giuseppe Tavani in his key study of mediaeval Galician-Portuguese poetry.

THE INFLUENCE OF FRANK CULTURE in the consolidation of the pilgrimage to Santiago de Compostela is easy to trace over the following centuries, as revealed by travellers' statements and pilgrims' chronicles. Bronseval, a secretary to the abbot of Clairvaux who travelled to Compostela in 1533 partly along the same route followed by the author of the *Codex Calixtinus*, noted that in Santiago "French is very common, as is Galician, and there are many Franks [*A lingua francesa é moi común, o mesmo do que a galega e abondan moito os francos*]." The comment is even more commendable due to the fact that he comes across many people he cannot communicate with, even the abbot of Armenteira who "was unable to chew the food of the Latin tongue [*era incapaz de mastigar o alimento da lingua latina*]," which was "a widespread complaint among Spaniards [*doenza moi espallada entre os españois*]" of the period.

SO IT IS HARD TO undervalue the massive pilgrimages that began in the eleventh century to the sarcophagus of the apostle Santiago from different parts of Europe, as captured in the *Codex Calixtinus*, the pilgrims' guide book. The road brought wayfarers to Compostela, but also builders and troubadours, books and learned monks. Theologians and teachers took different routes out of Santiago (although basically the French Road) and beyond the mountain passes, bound for Bologna or Salamanca. The city of Compostela was not so much an end of the road for concentric waves of European Christian culture, as a laboratory where that culture was transferred and transformed. As suggested by the *Codex Calixtinus*, Galicians were not peripheral, they were just remote, and of course their cultural level was higher than that of many peoples closer to France, which refuted the diffusion theory of culture, conceived as a succession of concentric rings starting from a central planet.

THE ECHOES FROM REGIONS BEYOND the mountain passes that reverberated powerfully in the times of archbishop Gelmírez and ricocheted beyond the Pyrenees would preserve the privileged relationship between Galician and European culture for centuries. The history

13 Alfonso X and his scribes [*Cantigas de Santa María*: TI 1 Cant. 1 f. 5r, detail]. Alfonso X "The Wise," 13th century

14 Making the dice from bone shards for the games "Hight Roll" & "As many on one as on two" [*Libro de los juegos*: TI 6 f. 65v, detail]. Alfonso X "The Wise," 1283

15 The jongleur in the knight court [*Cantigas de Santa María*: TI 1 Cant. 194 B f. 255v, detail]. Alfonso X "The Wise," 13th century

16 Journey to Emmaus at the Cloister of Santo Domingo de Silos [detail]. First Master of Santo Domingo de Silos, 12th century

of Galicia, a politically crippled kingdom that was nonetheless able to forge a high culture expressed in Romanesque art and anthologies of verse, contains many other such two-sided elements. The great masters who worked on the cathedral in Compostela were of Frank origin, or else, as in Mateo's case, strongly influenced by French culture and *pietàs*. Not to mention the poetic *corpus* of the anthologies, which established the cultural hegemony of a national poetic "school" and of a "genre," accepted as such by poets and troubadours of approximately half the peninsular area in the Castilian and the Portuguese courts, as pointed out by Italian scholar Giuseppe Tavani. The influence of the apostle's sanctuary would also be felt in the poetic irradiation that has existed for centuries. Mediaeval Galicia, the mores described by Otero, "was universal yet always found its own voice."

IV An Exit Through the Sailed Sea

Bearing in mind its identity traits and external image (and stereotype), Galicia has been considered a country of emigration or, in other words, as an "exit" by sea for millions of migrants who spread over half the American continent. In contrast with the limited land travels across pilgrims' routes, the conquest of the sea and mass emigration to America transformed the Atlantic Ocean into a huge lake continuously crossed by bodies and souls coming and going. Thanks to these migratory waves, the ethnic condition of Galicians became a telling sign for millions of immigrants of peninsular origin who settled in different Latin American countries, particularly Argentina and the Caribbean. The identification of Galicia abroad was produced first and foremost through the figure of the emigrant, the "*Gayegos*" as they were known in the slang of Buenos Aires, who spread a vague yet indelible trace of their native culture.

The conquest of the sea took place later, in the Middle Ages, but was systematic. The ancients' fear of the *mare tenebrosum* was genuine and yet was also a cultural construction that reinforced the idea of *finis terrae* or the end of the world. Navigation on that sea was characteristically coastal, although some accounts of sea voyages and links between the various land's ends and islands in western Europe—from Galicia to Brittany and Ireland—have survived, proving that that dark unknown sea was not totally uncharted. At a later date the Viking storeships and valiant Normans who began to arrive on Galician coasts by sea, with the self-assuredness of conquerors and the covetousness of the corsairs, marked the life of the inhabitants of this land for many years between the end of the first millennium and the beginning of the second millennium AD. Many were the prayers that bishop Gonzalo of Mondoñedo prayed

17 Queen Isabella of Portugal on a Pilgrimage to Santiago de Compostela [*Tavoa primeira dos Reyes de Portugal*: Add MS 12531 f. 9v]. Simon de Bening, 1530–1534

in order to sink the Norman ships in the Bay of Biscay, and equally important were the coastal fortresses such as the Towers of the West of the age of Gelmírez.

Since the discovery of the New World the sea has been a common and stable means of communication, yet one filled with uncertainties and dangers. The humanisation of the oceanic sea has only been possible in recent times, once the old ships driven by the force of the winds were gradually replaced by solid steam packets. For sea transport this meant the same revolution that iron had entailed for road transport. Thanks to this technological innovation, typical of Euro-American industrial expansion, the connections between Europe and the rest of the world grew tremendously. These relations favoured the exchange of goods but above all facilitated the movement of travellers. Some fifty million Europeans left the continent bound for overseas from the mid-nineteenth century to the period between the two world wars. Four fifths of this human flood went to America, chiefly to the north (the United States). Never before had the oceanic sea endured so much activity, nor would it do so again to such a degree.

And this is where we should situate the case of Galicia, as a part of this great European epic in which its inhabitants were displaced to America as emigrants. In the ten years between 1880 and 1890 Galicia became a region of mass emigration (i.e., its migratory rate was higher than four per thousand with respect to the total population), like many other European areas like the Italian Veneto or the Portuguese Minho. Net transoceanic emigration from Galicia was approximately just over two million people between 1830 and 1960, but the number of seafarers was considerably greater, given the high number of return journeys and the existence of phenomena such as temporary migrations, also known as "swallow migrations."

An enlightened priest, Ramón Castro López, whose parish was in Pantón in the region of Lugo, went so far as to say that his parishioners found it more convenient to go to Cuba than to the Saint Isidro fiestas in Madrid. That could have been a slight exaggeration, and yet without knowing one another Julio Camba would say much the same in his book *La rana viajera*, as did Vicente Risco in the presentation of the review *La Centuria*, where he declared that Ourense was six hundred kilometres away from Madrid and much closer to New York. And the same could have been said of Havana or Buenos Aires if Risco had paid more attention to emigration. All these statements were made in the early years of the twentieth century and were probably right, for moving to America was almost an obligation for any self-respecting Galician, even for the souls in Purgatory, who could travel more comfortably borne by the wind without having to pay for their ticket on the packets that docked every week in the Galician rias. At least that is what Fendetestas the bandit told Fiz Cotovelo, who appeared as a spirit from the beyond, to make sure he didn't disrupt his business in the forests of Cecebre, the *Bosque animado* in the writings of Wenceslao Fernández Flórez.

18 Fisterra Cape. 2009

19 Celtic ruins of Castro de Baroña, Porto do Son. C. 1st century BC

20 Valença do Minho. 2003

This daily contact between Galicia and the sea radically changed many aspects of life in Galicia. For a start, the emergence of its Atlantic cities, that grew parallel to the comings and goings in its ports. As well as fishing and cabotage ports, these became areas where the great European shipping companies, particularly English, French and German, periodically docked: the names *Royal Mail Line*, *Chargeurs Réunis* and *Hamburg America Line* became as familiar as the local stagecoach companies or the *Compañía Trasatlántica Española*, owned by the Marquise of Comillas. These cities managed to devote themselves completely to port activity, which in Vigo was considered a strategic option for the relations between Europe and America: some inhabitants of the city called their port "the door to Europe," just as residents of Lisbon had called the estuary of the Tajo.

Secondly, the motorway of the sea brought familiarity to the human and cultural relationships with South American cities and countries, which witnessed the comings and goings of so many thousands of migrants. Consular representatives proliferated, mostly in Vigo; the communications of seamen announced the arrivals and departures of packets; newspapers and magazines published at the time disseminated and even publicised facts and events that had taken place on this side of the sea or over yonder. From the first issues of reviews such as Vigo's *Vida Gallega*, first published in Vigo in 1909 and edited by journalist Jaime Solà, emigration was a key subject. The newspapers and journals printed in many Galician towns (suffice it to think of *El Emigrado* in A Estrada, or *Vivero en Cuba*), almost always defrayed by emigrants, became intermediaries between the two shores of the Atlantic, and also travelled along the ocean's motorway. Without emigration the appearance in Galicia of publications such as *Alfar* would have been impossible. On the initiative of the Uruguayan consul Julio Casal, *Alfar* became a symbol of the relations between Galicia and America. In the twenties, when the cultural modernisation of Mediterranean Europe focused on the connections with Paris, this end of Europe strengthened its ties with Buenos Aires, Montevideo and Havana (and on the rebound with Paris). Even the well known rumba *Para Vigo me voy*, composed by maestro Ernesto Lecuona in the thirties, revealed the great sentimental and popular value of the migratory waves between the "tip of Europe" and the "prows" of American ports.

V Farewells and Returns

"Galicia is a land of farewells [*Galicia é unha terra de adeuses*]," Otero Pedrayo solemnly declared. Galician wharfs are rife with laments and sorrows, both of those who depart, leaving a broken family behind them, and those who return defeated without as much as

21 *Cosulich Line Tireste: Espressi nord e sud America* [advertising poster]. A. Dondov, 1941

22 *Hamburg–Amerika Linie: L'Amazone, Les Antilles, L'Amérique du Nord* [advertising poster]. 1938

a handkerchief with which to dry their own tears. The same wharfs also witnessed great joys, which were not, however, described by the master from Trasalba, the joys of those who found *El Dorado* and were longing to get back to their hamlets to tell of the success their homeland had denied them. For Galicia is also a land of returns.

THIS PRESENCE OF AMERICAN LIFE in the everyday life of Galician society was the result of the migratory flood that came and went by the thousands every year. It was also produced by periodical publications, photographic portraits that were sent by migrants to their families shortly after their arrival, and the remittance of money from the remotest parts of the world by children to parents, husbands to wives, godparents to godchildren, brave young people to those who had loaned them the money for their fares. Emigration to America made Galicia a transcontinental land, divided into two large communities, one in each territory. The other side of the Atlantic was well informed of all that took place in the Galician atria and processions, just as Galicia was familiar with the movements in Sunday dances held by migrants' associations in Havana's *La Polar* or Buenos Aires' *Palermo*, where supposedly Galician products were consumed and tangos, rumbas and Cuban dances alternated with evocative Galician bagpipes.

SO THE MOTORWAY OF THE SEA was more than the packets of the *Royal Mail Line* and the third-class cabins occupied by peasants seeking beyond the seas the fortunes denied them in their homeland. The sea was also a channel for human and cultural relations, for sad farewells and happy reunions and, above all, for reciprocal influences. The sea was crossed by huge "packets" (as they were called by the writer from Riaxo) like the one that took Castelao as a child to La Boca neighbourhood in Buenos Aires, and also favoured the conveyance of news, feelings and even hopes through its mists. The nebulous carriers of the oceanic sea also welcomed the souls from Purgatory, who considered it their obligation to accompany the defeat of the packets and explain the visit of Death to families. News of births and deaths, infatuations and festivities came and went over the waves of the sea at the speed of a swallow. Even the souls in Purgatory communicated from the Recoleta and Chacarita cemeteries with their fellow souls in thousands of Galician cemeteries. Many people, a few brutes, less goods and of course many souls (although in this case we are not sure how many) would continuously cross the Atlantic Ocean from the late nineteenth century onwards, until the decline of emigration and new means of transport like aviation resulted in the disuse of a sea space that on the shores of Galicia would never be as humanised as it was at that time.

THE IDENTITY OF MODERN GALICIA had a strong American origin, for it was in those destinations—from Río de la Plata to the Caribbean—that thousands of Galician countrymen moved from the countryside to towns, where they acquired a certain degree of urban culture and above all learnt the value of education as a factor of social mobility

183

23 Parque Central &
Capitolo, La Havana. 1947

and recognition of their ethnic origin. Many succumbed to the process of assimilation, while others discovered that they came from a land that had a language of its own and a popular rural culture that deserved to be recovered and transformed. The fact that the leading figures of Galician culture like Manuel Curros Enríquez in Havana or Manuel Castro y López in Buenos Aires should have ended up settling in America indicates that Galician migration to America was socially transversal and culturally plural. Later on, during the Spanish Civil War, America once again became an easy haven for the many exiles devoted to the construction of Galician national culture: Luis Seoane and Lorenzo Varela in Argentina, Lois Tobío in Uruguay, Carlos Velo and Luis Soto in Mexico and Emilio González López and Ernesto Guerra da Cal in American universities. All they did was done thinking of Galicia and its collective future.

VI For a Bridge Culture

GEOGRAPHICAL POSITIONS AND HISTORICAL TRADITIONS are facts that help explain one of Galicia's most fruitful features in cultural geopolitics. Its spatial location has not helped this land to become a place of transit or a stage for border or territorial clashes. The construction of a road of pilgrimage has contributed to placing this European land's end in a central position, and the fact of being a *finis terrae* has made the ocean a well known and sailed sea and a link with America. The actual shaping of Galicia as a cultural nation has derived from the fact of being a "free port" between Europe and America. While Galician culture can be explained by its European roots, from Paulo Orosio to Otero Pedrayo, the experience of emigration and exile in America also proved decisive. Rafael María de Labra declared that "Galicia cannot be understood without America," in reference to the remittance of money, but we should not forget the cultural contributions made by figures like Luis Seoane, who envisaged a project for Galicia from his residence in Buenos Aires.

THE FACT OF HAVING BEEN a former kingdom in mediaeval Christian Europe and boasting a great cultural tradition forged around the Way of Saint James does not justify the present but it does help explain the cultural splendour of the twelfth and thirteenth centuries supremely expressed by the feeling and beauty of Romanesque architecture and the poetry of the anthologies of verse. This was a period of centrality in the European cultural space, a time when being at a land's end didn't mean being on the periphery. The smiling figure of the prophet Daniel, sculpted by master Mateo for the Portico of Glory of the basilica in Compostela, is the first such representation in mediaeval European sculpture, thereby proving the central position of Galicia in the Middle Ages.

24 The prophets Jeremiah, Daniel, Isaiah & Moses in the Portico of Glory at the Cathedral of Santiago de Compostela. C. 1188

THIS CULTURAL SPLENDOUR WAS ALSO reflected in Galician, a Romance language that co-existed with other Latin languages and which after the twelfth century evolved independently in the kingdom of Portugal, although it maintained many links with its origins in the lands of northern *Gallaecia*, especially with the city of Compostela, the chief centre of literary and artistic output. The perception of Galician as a specific Romance language for literature in the western peninsula has been a relatively recent development, although the use of "gallego" (Galician) as an adjective for the language first appeared in foreign texts such as the *Regles de trobar*, drawn up in Occitan in the late thirteenth century by Jofre de Foixà at the court of Sicily.[2]

WHETHER OR NOT THIS "GALICIAN" Romance should only be considered applicable to texts written in the present region of Galicia or in the totality of the former kingdom, including the new Portuguese kingdom which has extended to Alentejo, is a controversial issue in the social history of the language but it should not interfere with the key issue: the existence of an original linguistic unity, often summed up by the convenient expression "Galician-Portuguese" which, as a result of the political fragmentation of former *Gallaecia*, evolved in different ways north and south of the River Miño. The spoken and written language beyond the Miño evolved independently and looked to the Lisbon court, while the language this side of the river lacked political and institutional referents and by the Late Middle Ages began to be influenced by Castilian.

BE THAT AS IT MAY, in spite of the scarcity of written documents, the familiar everyday use of Galician by most of the population of Galicia during the so-called dark centuries enabled Romantic writers such as Rosalía de Castro to transform the way of speaking and popular traditions into refined expressions and a model for national literature. This recovery of the Galician language, even by those unfamiliar with the fertile mediaeval lyric tradition, did not only trigger the construction of a literary system but also strengthened the cultural and political relations between Galicia and Portugal and the culture expressed in Portuguese. At the time of the *Irmandades da Fala*, through Villar Ponte (Assembly of Lugo, November 1918) Portugal emerged as a positive model of reintegration for the construction of a Galician national project, for "As long as Portugal exists, Galicia will exist [*Mentres exista Portugal, existirá Galicia*]."

IN SPITE OF BEING SYSTEMATICALLY invoked by most of the members of the Galician cultural system, the ties between Galicia and culture expressed in Portuguese is far from being a practice personally and institutionally assumed, chiefly because of the linguistic reductionism to which these ties are subjected. We should obviously overcome this

---

2   H. Monteagudo, *Historia social da lingua galega* (Vigo: Galaxia, 1999).

25 Cathedral of Santiago de Compostela.
2005

26 Torres Hejduk, City of Culture of Galicia
& Cathedral of Santiago de Compostela.
Manuel G. Vicente, 2010

impasse designing new strategies for the future of Galician culture. One such strategy is undoubtedly taking better advantage of this bridge between sister cultures and languages on several continents, particularly America. This would entail reformulating the position of Galician culture as regards Portuguese culture and Galician culture produced in Castilian. Although this statement might be slightly unorthodox, it could also invoke a dense cultural tradition of Galician figures (and even of non-national figures) who have shared and maintained this standpoint. We should bear in mind that such stances were usually upheld by Galicians who had emigrated or had been forced into exile for political reasons.

SUFFICE IT TO THINK OF Alfonso Castelao, whose "river-book" *Sempre en Galiza* contains numerous reflections on the new political concept of "Hespanha," that overcomes the traditional disputes between Castilla and Portugal. In the opinion of Castelao, as in those of many Spanish and Portuguese authors of the time (such as Maragall, Valera or Unamuno, but also Teófilo Braga, Oliveira Martins or Teixeira de Pascoaes, not to mention Saramago, recently deceased), there is an obvious difference between Castilian and Hispanic (or Spanish) culture which for a long time even comprised the culture expressed in Portuguese. Another factor, besides this permeability, is the existence in Galicia of an important literary tradition in Castilian that transcends the promotion of the language and has led authors like Valentín Paz-Andrade to maintain that Galicia is a "nursemaid to two cultures" in which he placed Valle-Inclán next to Cabanillas and Castelao.[3]

RECENT STUDIES AND EDUCATIONAL STRATEGIES regarding the future of Iberian languages, chiefly from Brazil, are opening up a path for future development that entails a great challenge. This path consists of promoting the permeability between the two great transcontinental Iberian languages that will transform the present rivalry and even forced differences into convergent knowledge or at least a mutual and passive understanding and a growing use of both in areas such as science, diplomacy, business or tourism, until recently dominated by English as a "hyper-language." This is in fact quite a long path that depends on different commitments. However, it does present a number of positive elements in cultural terms and even as regards the Galician language which I would like to mention to conclude this historical *promenade*. Galicia's cultural splendour coincided with the periods in which it had occupied a relatively central position within European Christian civilisation, mediating between the two great Iberian languages and cultures. This new course of history may well allow it once again to take centre stage in a cosmopolitan and global future through which it will still have to sail in its own ships. It may be a dream or a utopia, but nothing can exist without having been previously envisaged.

---

3   V. Paz-Andrade, *Galicia como tarea* (Buenos Aires: Centro Gallego de Buenos Aires, 1959).

SIGFRIED GIEDION

ON
MONUMENTALITY

Sigfried Gideon

"Part 2. On Monumentality: 'Marginalia' & 'Nine Points on Monumentality'"

Architecture, You and Me. The Diary of a Development. Cambridge, MA: Harvard University Press, 1958

"The Need for a New Monumentality"

New Architecture and City Planning. A Symposium. Paul Zucker, ed. New York: Philosophical Library, 1944

Marginalia

One day in New York, in 1943, Fernand Léger the painter, José Luis Sert the architect and town planner (later to become Dean of the Graduate School of Design, Harvard University), and I met together. We discovered that each of us had been invited to write an article for a publication to be prepared by the American Abstract Artists. After discussion, we thought it would be more interesting if we all discussed the same topic, each approaching it from the point of view of his own field of activity: the painter, the architect, and the historian. We decided upon the subject, "A New Monumentality," and finally assembled our joint views under nine heads, which are here printed for the first time.

The publication of the American Abstract Artists never materialised. My contribution, titled "The New Monumentality," appeared later, in the collection of papers, *New Architecture and City Planning.*[1]

---

1 *New Architecture and City Planning. A Symposium.* Paul Zucker, ed (New York: Philosophical Library, 1944), 547–68

Many friends whose opinion I value shook their heads at the use of so dangerous a term, and one to which the ruling taste had given so banal a meaning. They were right. It was certainly dangerous to revive a term that had become so debased. Lewis Mumford, in a *New Yorker* article, took up a defensive position. Despite these warnings, I lectured on this topic in many places in the United States, and also, later, on the other side of the Atlantic.

All of us are perfectly aware of the fact that monumentality is a dangerous thing, especially at a time when most people do not even grasp the most elementary requirements for a functional building. But we cannot close our eyes. Whether we want it or not, the problem of monumentality still lies before us as the task of the immediate future. All that could then be done was to point out some of the dangers of some of the possibilities.

Following a lecture in the Royal Institute of British Architects, London, on September 26, 1946, the *Architectural Review* (London) decided "to take the matter a stage further" and, in their issue of September 1948, some of the world's leading architects and architectural writers defined what monumentality meant to them, and where they thought it fitted into the twentieth-century architectural picture. Contributions came from Georg Paulsson (Uppsala, Sweden), Henry Russel Hitchcock (Smith College, USA), William Holford (London), Walter Gropius (then at Harvard), Lucio Costa (Rio de Janeiro) and Alfred Roth (Zurich), and myself. Lewis Mumford followed this up with an essay, "Monumentalism, Symbolism and Style," in the *Architectural Review*. One can willingly agree with Mumford's plaint: "Now we live in an age which has not merely abandoned a great many historic symbols, but has likewise made an effort to deflate the symbol itself by denying the values which it represents ... Because we have dethroned symbolism, we are now left, momentarily, with but a single symbol of almost universal validity: that of the machine ... What we are beginning to witness today is a reaction against this distorted picture of modern civilization."

"The monument," he adds, "is a declaration of love and admiration attached to the higher purposes men hold in common ... An age that has deflated its values and lost sight of its purposes will not produce convincing monuments."[2]

This is certainly true for the monuments of the ruling taste, but is not just when speaking of the work of the creative artists of our time such as Brancusi, Antoine Pevsner, Hans Arp, Naum Gabo, Alberto Giacometti, or Picasso.

These all desire nothing more ardently than to see their work placed on the public streets, or squares, or in parks—in the midst of the people. Up to now, however, the administrators and leaders of the ruling taste have banished almost all their products to museums and to private collections, and kept them there behind bolts and bars.

2 Lewis Mumford, "Monumentalism, Symbolism and Style," *Architectural Review* (London: April 1949): 179.

The Need for a
New Monumentality

Modern architecture had to take the hard way. Tradition had been mercilessly misused by the representatives of ruling academic taste in all fields concerned with emotional expression.

The buildings of perennial power such as the Acropolis, the sensitive construction of Gothic cathedrals, the geometric phantasy of Renaissance churches, and the exquisite scale of eighteenth-century squares were all in existence.

But they could not help. For the moment they were dead. They had become temporarily frozen in the icy atmosphere created by those architects and their patrons who, in order to compensate for their own lack of expressive force, had misused eternal names by pilfering from history.

In this way the great monumental heritages of mankind became poisonous to everybody who touched them. Behind every great building of the past leered the faces of its misusers.

This was the period of *pseudomonumentality*. The greater part of the nineteenth century belongs to it. Its models of the past were not imbued, as in the Renaissance, with a strong artistic vision leading to new results. There was an undirected helplessness and, at the same time, a routine use of shapes from bygone periods. These were used indiscriminately everywhere, for any kind of building. Because they had lost their inner significance they had become devaluated; mere *clichés* without emotional justification. *Clichés* cannot be used by creative artists, only by professional eclectics. Thus the creative spirit had to be banished wherever public taste was being formed. Those obedient servants of the ruling taste have now devaluated and undermined the taste and the emotions of the public and brought about the extreme banalisation which still exists today.

Periods which are dear to our memory, whose structures and work rose beyond their mere temporal existence, were aware that monumentality, because of its inherent character, can be employed but rarely, and then only for the highest purposes. In ancient Greece monumentality was used sparingly, and then only to serve the gods, or, to a certain extent, the life of the community. The Easterly discrimination and discipline of the Greeks in this respect is one of the reasons for their lasting influence.

Contemporary architecture takes the hard way

Contemporary architecture had to take the hard way. As with painting and sculpture, it had to begin anew. It had to reconquer the most primitive things, as if nothing had ever been done before. It could not return to Greece, to Rome, or to the Baroque, to be conforted by their experience. In certain crises man must live in seclusion, to become aware of his own inner feelings and thoughts. This was the situation for all the arts around 1910.

Architects found traces of the undisguised expression of their period in structures far removed from monumental edifices. They found them in market halls, in factories, in the bold vaults of the great exhibition buildings, or in the only real monument of this period, the Eiffel Tower, 1889. There was no denying that these lacked the splendour of buildings of bygone periods, which had been nourished by handicraft and a long tradition. They were naked and rough, but they were honest. Nothing else could have served as the point of departure for a language of our time.

Three steps of contemporary architecture

Architecture is not concerned exclusively with construction.

First, architecture has to provide an adequate frame for man's intimate surroundings. Individual houses as well as the urban community have to be planned from the human point of view.

Modern architecture had to begin with the single cell, with the smallest unit, the low-cost dwelling, which to the last century had seemed beneath the talents and attention of the artist. The 1920's and 1930's saw a resurgence of research in this direction, for it seemed then senseless to push ahead before first trying to find new solutions for this task.

The main impetus lay in the fact that this problem also involved social and human orientation. But, looking back, we can see that an architecture which had to begin anew found here a problem where the utmost care had to be given to exact organisation within the smallest space, and to the greatest economy of means. Of course, at the same time, houses were built for the middle or upper classes where, for the first time, a new space conception could be carried out. But it was housing for the lower-income classes that taught the architects the exactitude of planning which had been lost in the nineteenth century.

The second step: From the human point of view, and from the architectonic view as well, houses and blocks are not isolated units. They are incorporated in urban settlements and these are parts of a greater entity, the city. An architect who is not interested in the whole scope of planning, from the right height of a kitchen sink to the layout of a region, in not part of the contemporary building scene. From the single cell, to the neighbourhood, the city, and the organisation of the whole region is one direct sequence. Thus it can be said that the second phase of modern architecture was concentrated on urbanism.

The third step lies ahead. In view of what has happened in the last century and because of the way modern architecture has come into being it is the most dangerous and the most difficult step. This is the reconquest of monumental expression.

People desire buildings that represent their social, ceremonial, and community life. They want these buildings to be more than a functional fulfilment. They seek the expression of their aspirations in monumentality, for joy and for excitement.

In the United States, where modern architecture has had up to now (1944) a rather limited influence because it has been more or less confined to single-family dwellings, housing projects, factories, and office buildings, it may perhaps seem too early to speak about these problems. But things are moving fast. In countries where modern architecture has been recently called upon for solutions of museums, theatres, universities, churches, or concert halls, it has been forced to seek the monumental expression which lies beyond functional fulfilment. If it cannot meet this demand, the whole development will be in mortal danger of a new escape into academicism.

Monumentality—an eternal need

Monumentality springs from the eternal need of people to create symbols for their activities and for their fate or destiny, for their religious beliefs and for their social convictions.

Every period has the impulse to create symbols in the form of monuments, which, according to the Latin meaning, are "things that remind," things to be transmitted to later generations. This demand for monumentality cannot, in the long run, be suppressed. It will find an outlet at all costs.

Pseudomonumentality

Our period is no exception. For the present it continues the habits of the last century and follows in the tracks of pseudomonumentality. No spacial political or economic system is to blame for this. No matter how different they may be in their political and economic orientations, whether the most progressive or the most reactionary, there is one point where the governments of all countries meet: in their conception of monumentality.

Pseudomonumentality has nothing to do with Roman, Greek, or any other style or tradition. It came into being within the orbit of Napoleonic society which imitated the manner of a former ruling class.

Napoleon represents the model that gave the nineteenth century its form: the self-made man who became inwardly uncertain.

The origin of pseudomonumental buildings can be found in the paper architecture and lifeless schemes that later became reality everywhere.

A prototype is the scheme for a museum by Jean Nicolas Louis Durand (1860–1934), illustrated in his lectures *Précis de leçons d'architecture* (1801–1805) which were many times translated and reprinted and were used by architects of every country. His lectures are forgotten today, but the buildings which resulted from their study are still standing and new ones have been added in a continuous stream for 140 years. The recipe is always the same: take some curtains of columns and put them in front of any building, whatever its purpose and whatever the consequences.

One could compile an immense square of "monumental edifices" of the whole world, erected in recent years, from the Hall of German Art, 1937, in Munich or the Mellon Institute, 1937, in Pittsburgh, to recent museums in Washington, or similar buildings in Moscow.

The palace of the League of Nations in Geneva (finished 1935) is perhaps the most distinguished example of internationally brewed eclecticism. The moral cowardice reflected in its architecture seems to have an almost prophetic affinity to the failure of the League itself.

How can this be explained?

Those who govern and administer may be the most brilliant men in their fields, but in their emotional or artistic training, they reflect the average man of our period, plagued as he is by the rift between his methods of thinking and his methods of feeling. The thinking may be developed to a very high level, but the emotional background has not caught up with it. It is still imbued with the pseudo-ideals of the nineteenth century. Is it, then, any wonder that most official artistic judgments are disastrous, or that the decisions made for urban planning, monuments, and public buildings are without contact with the real spirit of the period?

The lost sense of monumentality

Periods of real cultural life had always the capacity to project creatively their own image of society. They were able to build up their community centres (agora, forum, mediaeval square) to fulfill this purpose.

Our period, up to now, has proved itself incapable of creating anything to be compared with these institutions. There are monuments, many monuments, but where are the community centres? Neither radio nor television can replace the personal contact which alone can develop community life.

All this is easily recognisable, but accusations alone do not help. We have to ask: What can be done?

The question of how to keep the people from going further astray cannot easily be solved. Only complete frankness will be of any use, frankness on both sides, of those who have to re-create the lost sense for monumentality, and those who will profit by it; of the artist on the one hand, and the client on the other.

We outlined the reasons why architecture had to cut itself off from the past, and why architects had to concentrate on functional problems and to re-educate themselves through them. This had its consequences.

Dind't the new architects tend to ignore the higher aspirations of the people? That this danger still exists cannot be denied. In countries where modern architecture has won the battle and been entrusted with monumental tasks involving more than functional problems, one cannot but observe that something is lacking in the buildings executed.[3] "Something" is an inspired architectural imagination able to satisfy the demand for monumentality. What is more, architects, sculptors, and painters have become unaccustomed to working together. They have lost contact with each other. There is no collaboration. Why? Because all three have been banished from the great public tasks.

The community's emotional life

The situation of today's modern painter differs in many respects from that of the avant-gardists of the late nineteenth century. Paul Cézanne was proud, when he could sell one of his pictures for 100 francs. Today, many private and public collections are filled with the paintings of Picasso, Braque, Léger, Miró, and others. Modern art is regarded as a sure investment and America owns the most important collections.

But in one respect the situation remains unchanged: art is still regarded as luxury, and not as the medium to shape the emotional life in the broadest sense.

Only in exceptional cases (for example, Picasso's *Guernica* in 1937) have creative contemporary artists been allowed to participate in a community task. Precious artistic forces, capable of providing the symbols for our period, linger unused—as in the nineteenth century when Edouard Manet vainly offered to paint free of charge a mural depicting the real life of Paris on the walls of the City Hall.

Yes, the best known artists today sell well, but there are no walls, no places, no buildings, where their talents can touch the great public; where they can form the people and the people can form them.

Again and again it has been reiterated that modern art cannot be understood by the public. We are not sure that this argument is

---

3 This was written in 1944; compare Part 6, written in 1954 and 1956.

absolutely correct. We only know that those who govern and administer public taste are without the necessary emotional understanding.

Is the artist estranged from life? There are several resons to believe that he is not. But the artist has been unable to do anything about it because he has been artificially expelled from direct contact with the community.

There are reasons to believe that the modern artists are right. Remember that, poor and rich, under the domination of the press, academy, and governments were always wrong in their taste and judgment, and that all the offical art of that period appears so ridiculous today that the museums no longer show it to the public. Those artists, on the other hand, who had been driven into seclusion, reveal the creative spirit which permeated the nineteenth century.

The same situation exists today. Nothing has changed in this respect. I have seen in painting, sculpture, architecture, and poetry, a long row of artistic leaders (by this I mean those who shape our emotional life) living their isolated existence, far from the public and the understanding of those who could have brought them in touch with the community. How is it possible to develop an art "satisfying" to the people when those who personify the creative forces are not allowed to work upon the living body of our period?

Not the imitator, only the imaginative creator is fitted to build our absent centres of social life which can awake the public once more to their old love for festivals, and incorporate movement, colour, new materials, and our abundant technical possibilities. Who else could utilise these means to open up new ways for invigorating community life?

I am not aware of any period but our own which, to such a frightening extent, has wasted its few available creative forces.

The demand for a decent social life for all has finally been recognised, alter more than a century's fight.

The demand for shaping the emotional life of the masses is still unrecognised. Regarded as inessential this is laid mostly in the hand of speculators.

Painting points the way

Painting, the most sentient of the visual arts, has often forecast things to come.

It was painting which first realised the spatial conception of our period and discovered methods of representing it.

Later, in the thirties, by these same artistic means, the horror of the war to come was foreshadowed many years before it came, when, for instance, Picasso around 1930 painted his figures with strange abbreviations and sometimes terrifying lines which most of us did not understand until these forms and expressions were verified by later events. His *Monument in Wood* (1930) may serve to illustrate this phenomenon.

It is a sketch for a modern sculpture of enormous scale. Picasso did not specify for what purpose these 1930 studies for a monument were meant. But it is now clear that these sketches forecast the reality, and the inherent significance of the symbol did not reaveal itself until later.

It symbolises our attitude toward the war (of 1939–1945). It does not glorify war in a heroic gesture, as the Napoleonic Arc de Triomphe of the Place de l'Etoile. It stands as a memorial to the horror of this period and of its tragic conflict: the knowledge that mechanised killing is not the way to solve human problems, but that nevertheless it has to be done.

It is frightening. It tells the thruth. It has the *terribilita* that—for his contemporaries—emanated from Michelangelo's late sculptures, a terrifying threat which Picasso translates into present-day language.

Now, at a moment when we are living in blood and horror, painting announces another period. This is the re-birth of the lost sense of monumentality.

One trend can be observed in recent years, common to nearly all of the leading painters. Together with the urge for larger canvases, brighter colours have appeared, full of inherent hope. At the same time there is an impulse toward simplification. This has ocurred after a development of three decades during which modern painting has become ripe for great tasks. Great and unresolved complexes have had to be expressed in the shortest, most direct way. What began as necessary structural abbreviations now emerge as symbols. The work of Arp, Miró, Léger, and many others is moving in this direction.

Modern artists have created these symbols out of the anonymous forces of our period. Nobody asked for them, they have just appeared. They have no factual content, no significance at the moment other than emotional response. They are not for those whose emotional life is still imbued with the last century's official taste. But children can understand them, because these figurations are as close to primitive life as they are to our complicated civilization.

For the first time in centuries artists have returned to the simplicity which is the hallmark of any kind of symbolic expression. They have shown that the elements indispensable for monumentality are available. They have acquired the rare power of a mural language.

Once more painting may forecast the next development in architecture. But not only in architecture; it may forecast a newly integrated life, far removed from the devastating idolatry of production.

Great changes are necessary in many spheres to accomplish this demand; and not least in the emotional domain. This is the moment when painting, sculpture, and architecture should come together on a basis of common perception, aided by all the technical means which our period has to offer.

Corn is planted for the winter. Wars have been prepared in peace. Why should no peace be prepared in war? The means for a more dignified life must be prepared before the demand arises. Will these means be utilised?

Technical and emotional means

There is an enormous backlog of new means and unused possibilities held in reserve by engineers and inventors of all kinds. At the same time there exists a tragic inability to use these treasures and to merge them into our human emotional needs. No period has had so many means and such a lack of ability to use them.

In one of his essays, T. S. Eliot says the seventeenth-century poets "possessed a mechanism of sensibility which could devour any kind of experience."[4] Their emotional and their mental apparatus functioned like communicating tubes. Technical and scientific experiences inevitably found their emotional counterpart, as is revealed in the artistic creations of that period. This is just what we lack. Today this direct contact, this coherence between feeling and thinking, has vanished.

Now, after the great horror of our period, age-old, perennial problems arise again. We have banned from life the artistic expression for joy and festivities. Both have to be incorporated into human existence and are as necessary for our equilibrium as food and housing. That we have become incapable of creating

---

4 T. S. Eliot, "The Metaphysical Poets," *Selected Essays 1917–1932* (New York: Harcourt & Brace, 1932), 247.

monuments and festivals and that we have lost all feeling for the dignity of urban centres is tied up with the fact that our emotional life has been regarded as unessential and as a purely private affair. Behold the patterns of present-day cities!

Urban centres and spectacles

Urban centres will originate when cities are not regarded as mere agglomerations of jobs and traffic lights. They will arise when men become aware of the isolation in which they live in the midst of a turbulent crowd, and when demand for a fuller life—which means community life—becomes irresistible. Community life is closely connected with an understanding of relaxation, with the urge for another vitalising influence besides the job and the family —an influence capable of expanding men's narrow private existence.

No great civilisation has existed which has not fulfilled man's irrepressible longing for institutions where such broader life can develop. In different periods these institutions have had different aims, but, whether called the Greek gymnasium or agora, the Roman *thermae* or *forum*, the mediaeval cathedrals or market places, all have contributed to the development of human values. These institutions were never conceived of as financial investments. Their function was not to produce money or to bolster up a waning trade.

The urban centre of the coming period will never be a neighbour to slums. It should not be financed by bond issues on the basis that its cost will be self-liquidating within a period of years. The means must come from the community.

Community centres? What has the economist to say about the large expenditures involved in their building?

The hope of our period is that diverse groups are moving unconsciously in parallel directions. The liberal economists, such as John Maynard Keynes, are stressing the fact that economic equilibrium can only be obtained by a surplus production not destined for daily use. Goods must be produced which cannot be conceived of in terms of profit of loss, suply and demand. Keynes does not speak of urban centres, he deals with the theory of employment and money. He observes that today the necessary large-scale expenditures for non-consumable goods are only admissible in the case of catastrophes such as earthquakes, war, or "digging holes in the ground known as gold-mining which adds nothing to the real wealth of the world. The education of our statesmen on the principles of classical economics stands in the way of anything better."[5] Why not keep the economic machinery going by creating urban centres?

The problem ahead of us focuses on the question: Can the emotional apparatus of the average man be reached? Is he susceptible only to football games and horse races? We do not believe it. There are forces inherent in man, which come to the surface when one evokes them. The average man, with a century of falsified emotional education behind him, may not be won over suddenly by the contemporary symbol in painting and sculpture. But his inherent, though unconscious, feeling may slowly be awakened by the original expression of a new community life. This can be done within a framework of urban centres and in great spectacles capable of fascinating the people.

Anyone who had occasion during the Paris Exhibition of 1937 to observe the hundreds of thousands lined up in the summer evenings along the banks of the Seine and on the Trocadero bridge, quietly waiting for the spectacles of fountains, light, sound, and fireworks, knows that the persistent predisposition for dramatic representation, even in the form of abstract elements, has not been lost. There is no difference in this respect between Europe and

---

5 J. M. Keynes, *The General Theory of Employment Interest and Money* (New York & London: Palgrave Macmillan, 1936), 129

America. In 1939, at the New York World's Fair, when aerial plays of water, light, sound, and fireworks were thrown into the sky, a sudden spontaneous applause arose.

Everybody is susceptible to symbols. Our period is no exception. But those who govern must know that spectacles, which will lead the people back to a neglected community life, must be reincorporated within urban centres—those very centres which our mechanised civilisation has always regarded as inessential. Not haphazard world's fairs, which in their present form have lost their old significance, but newly created urban centres should be the site for collective emotional events, where the people play as important a role as the spectacle itself, and where a unity of the architectural background, the people, and the symbols conveyed by the spectacles, will be achieved.

[...]

NINE POINTS ON MONUMENTALITY
(Written by Josep Lluís Sert, Fernand Léger
and Sigfried Giedion)

Que donneriez vous ma belle
Pour revoir votre mari?
Je donnerai Versailles,
Paris et Saint Denis
Les tours de Notre Dame
Et le clocher de mon pays.
Auprès de ma blonde
Qu'il fait bon, fait bon, fait bon.

From an old French song, *Auprès de ma blode*

1. Monuments are human landmarks which men have created as symbols for their ideals, for their aims, and for their actions. They are intended to outlive the period, which originated them,

and constitute a heritage for future generations. As such, they form a link between the past and the future.

2. Monuments are the expression of man's highest cultural needs. They have to satisfy the eternal demand of the people for translation of their collective force into symbols. The most vital monuments are those which express the feeling and thinking of this collective force—the people.

3. Every bygone period which shaped a real cultural life had the power and the capacity to create these symbols. Monuments are, therefore, only possible in periods in which a unifying consciousness and unifying culture exist. Periods which exist for the moment have been unable to create lasting monuments.

4. The last hundred years have witnessed the devaluation of monumentality. This does not mean that there is any lack of formal monuments or architectural examples pretending to serve this purpose: but the so-called monuments of recent date have, with rare exceptions, become empty shells. They in no way represent the spirit or the collective feeling of modern times.

5. This decline and misuse of monumentality is the principal reason why modern architects have deliberately disregarded the monument and revolted against it.

Modern architecture, like modern painting and sculpture, had to start the hard way. It began by tackling the simpler problems, the more utilitarian buildings like low-rent housing, schools, office buildings, hospitals, and similar structures. Today modern architects know that buildings cannot be conceived as isolated units, that they have to be incorporated into the vaster urban schemes. There are no frontiers between architecture and town planning, just as there are no frontiers between the city and the region. Correlation between them is necessary. Monuments should constitute the most powerful accents in these vast schemes.

6. A new step lies ahead. Post-war changes in the whole economic structure of nations may bring with them the organisation of community life in the city which has been practically neglected up to date.

7. The people want the buildings that represent their social and community life to give more than functional fulfilment. They want their aspiration for monumentality, joy, pride and excitement to be satisfied.

The fulfilment of this demand can be accomplished with the new means of expression at hand, though it is no easy task. The following conditions are essential for it: A monument being the integration of the work of the planner, architect, painter, sculptor, and landscapist demands close collaboration between all of them. This collaboration has failed in the last hundred years. Most modern architects have not been trained for this kind of integrated work. Monumental tasks have not been entrusted to them.

As a rule, those who govern and administer a people, brilliant as they may be in their special fields, represent the average man of our period in their artistic judgements. Like this average man, they experience a split between their methods of thinking and their methods of feeling. The feeling of those who govern and administer the countries is untrained and still imbued with the pseudo-ideals of the nineteenth century. This is the reason why they are not able to recognise the creative forces of our period, which alone could build the monuments or public buildings that should be integrated into new urban centres which can form a true expression for our epoch.

8. Sites for monuments must be planned. This will be possible once replanning is undertaken on a large scale which will create vast open spaces in the now decaying areas of our cities. In these open spaces, monumental architecture will find its appropriate

setting which now does not exist. Monumental buildings will then be able to stand in space, for, like trees or plants, monumental buildings cannot be crowded in upon any odd lot in any district. Only when this space is achieved can the new urban centres come to life.

9. Modern materials and new techniques are at hand: light metal structures; curved, laminated wooden arches; panels of different textures, colours, and sizes; light elements like ceilings which can be suspended from big trusses covering practically unlimited spans.

Mobile elements can constantly vary the aspect of the buildings. These mobile elements, changing positions and casting different shadows when acted upon by wind or machinery, can be the source of new architectural effects.

During night hours, colour and forms can be projected on vast surfaces. Such displays could be projected upon buildings for purposes of publicity or propaganda. These buildings would have large plane surfaces planned for this purpose, surfaces which are non-existent today.

Such big animated surfaces with the use of colour and movement in a new spirit would offer unexplored fields to mural painters and sculptors.

Elements of nature, such as trees, plants, and water, would complete the picture. We could group all these elements in architectural ensembles: the stones which have always been used, the new materials which belong to our times, and colour in all its intensity which has long been forgotten.

Man-made landscapes would be correlated with nature's landscapes and all elements combined in terms of the new and vast *façade*, sometimes extending for many miles, which has been revealed to us by the air view. This could be contemplated not only during a rapid flight but also from a helicopter stopping in mid-air.

Monumental architecture will be something more than strictly functional. It will have regained its lyrical value. In such monumental layouts, architecture and city planning could attain a new freedom and develop new creative possibilities, such as those that have begun to be felt in the last decades in the fields of painting, sculpture, music, and poetry.

Cidade da Cultura de Galicia I 2010

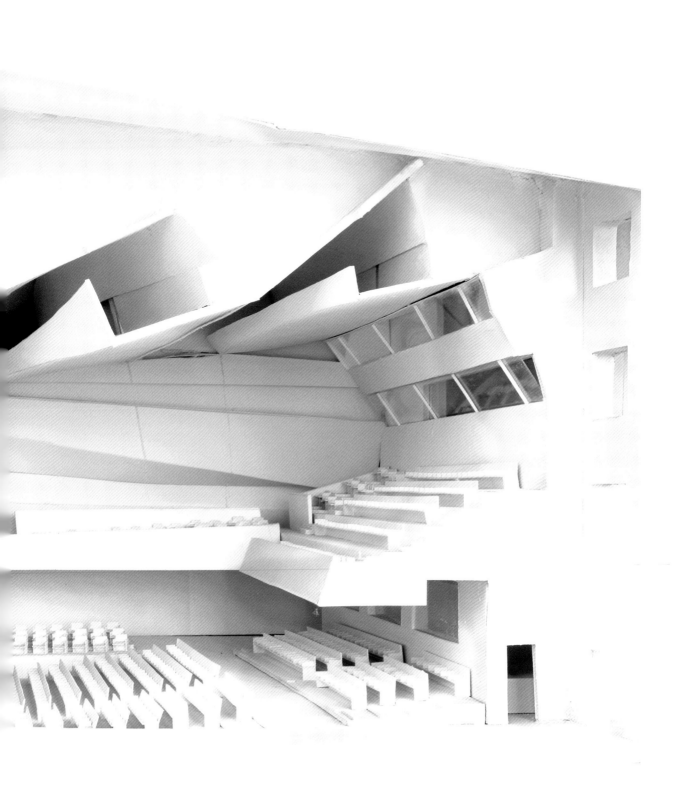

Cidade da Cultura de Galicia IV 2010

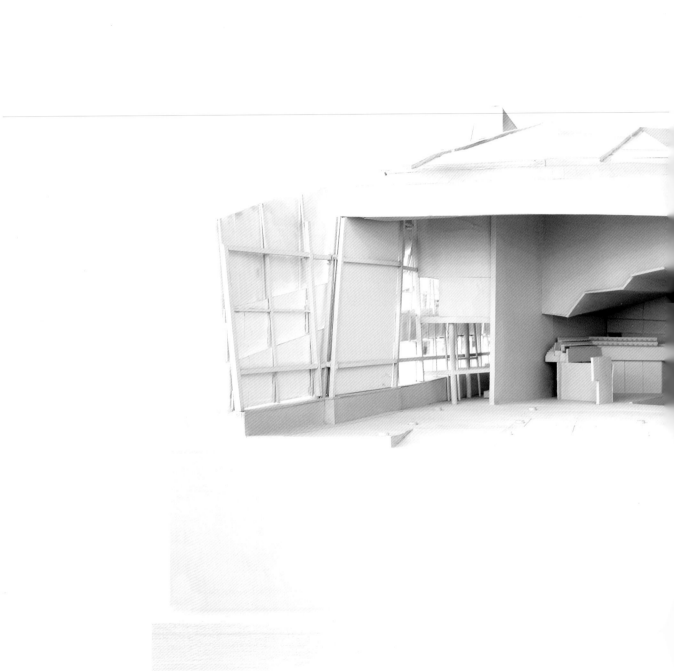

Cidade da Cultura de Galicia III 2010

Biographical Notes

Maxwell L. Anderson

IMA~Indianapolis Museum of Art
Director

He received an A.B. from Dartmouth College (1977), and A.M. (1978) and Ph.D. (1981) degrees in Art History from Harvard University. His career began at MET~The Metropolitan Museum of Art in 1981, serving for five year as its assistant curator of Greek and Roman Art. Since 1987 he has directed several art museums, including The Whitney Museum of American Art (1998–2003). During his tenure in IMA~Indianapolis Museum of Art since May 2006, Anderson has turned the institution into a world-wide bastion, specially with regard to the ethical collecting of antiquities, institutional transparency, artists' rights, and uses of new technologies in museums of the future. In 1990 he was decorated with the rank of *Commendatore dell'Ordine al Merito della Repubblica Italiana.*

Lawrence Chua

Cornell University
Professor, History of Architecture and Urbanism

His researches has been focused on the relation between Architecture and the construction of the social identity with well-known dissertation works as *Holidays in the Sun: Architecture, violence, and the aesthetics of leisure in Thailand from 1911 to 1976* or *Ambivalent Modernity: Instabilities of the imperial project in the Empire Stadium at Wembley during the early 20th century.* He is as well a regular contributor on peridicals like *Art&Text, Artforum, Flash Art* or *Frieze,* and his writings on the field of visual arts could be found on publications as *Vitamin P. Contemporary Painters* (Phaidom, 2003) or *Julie Mehretu, Black City* (Hatje Cantz, 2006). In addition he has published his first novel under the title of *Gold by the Inch: a novel* (Grove Press, 1998).

Rachel Healy

SOH~Sidney Opera House
Director, Performing Arts

Prior to her appointment in August 2006 as Director of Performing Arts from the SOH~Sidney Opera House, Rachel Healy worked as General Manager of companies as The Australian Ballet, Handspan Theatre, Magpie Theatre, State Theatre Company of South Australia, or Company B from Belvoir Street Theatre. In addition, she has server on a number of art boards, including Legs on the Wall, Arst Industry Council, Kage Physical Theatre, and Live Performance Australia. En 1998 she was awarded the Nugget Coombs Award for Arts Administration in the Young Manager category. In November 2010, Healy has extended here activities to the private sector forming the agency Rachel Healy & Associates, from which she supports, advises, and produces for different performing arts companies and institutions.

Ismail Serageldin

Library of Alexandria
Director

He received an A.B. in Science in Engineering from Cairo University (1964) and Ph.D from Harvard University (1972). He has developed and intense professional career in the World Bank along almost thirty years, with special mention to the programs that, under his direction, approached the management of water sources in Africa and Middle East. Since his appointment as Director of the Library of Alexandria in March 2001 and its official opening of the cultural complex in April 2002, Serageldin has continued developing his knowledge on biotechnology, rural development, sustainability and the value of science in society. Committed with the best understanding between the West and the Arab World, Serageldin is member of the High-level Group of Alliance of Civilizations.

Ramón Villares

Consello da Cultura Galega
Presidente

He received an A.B. (1973), and Ph.D. (1980) in History from USC~Universidade de Santiago de Compostela. Since 1987, Villares is Chair of Contemporary History of the School of Geography and History, where he has been as well firstly the Dean (1986–1990), and later the President (1990–1994) on the university where he was formed. In addition, is founding member and president (1996–2002) of the Spanish Association of Contemporary History, and author of reference publications as *La propiedad de la tierra en Galicia, 1500–1936* (Siglo XXI, 1982), *Galicia. A Historia* (Galaxia, 1984), or *El mundo contemporáneo, siglos XXI y XX* (Taurus, 2001). Since 2006 is numerary member of the RAG~Real Academia Galega and held the position of President of the Consello da Cultura Galega.

Candida Höfer

Photographer

The oeuvre of Candida Höfer—along with the works of Andreas Gursky, Axel Hütte, Thomas Ruff and Thomas Struth—is framed within the tradition of German photographers, direct heirs to the conceptual aesthetic and teachings of Bernd and Hilla Becher at the Düsseldorfer Kunstakademie, who would readapt the original project of the New Objectivity to adopt a unique way to face the world. Her photographs show an amost ethnographic interest in the multiple forms of representation present in contemporary culture, specially those where the knowledge developing occurs, such as museums, churches, theatres, archives and libraries. Her work has been shown on *Documenta 11* (Kasel, 2002) or on the 2003 edition of the Venice Biennale along with Martin Kippenberger. During 2010 has produced the project entitled *Spaces of Their Own* for the Galician institution Xacobeo.

Illustration Credits

Special thanks for the trust, assistance, support and dedication of the following people, without whom this book and the exhibition would not have been possible.

Michele Abate
Elvira Allocati
Maxwell L. Anderson
Shady Arafa
Jillian Ballard
Valentina Bandelloni
Francesco Baragiola
Cassie Browne
Federica Brivio
Peter Brook
Herbert Burkert
Nadia Casas
Emma Cavazzini
Valeria Cecconello
Lawrence Chua
Fátima Díez
Silvia Domínguez
Rania El Bahtimi
Emma Falque
Marcello Francone
Elena Gaiardelli
Sergio Gómez
Rachel Healy
Candida Höfer
Scarlett R. Huffman
Rachel Huizinga
Anne Jump
María Kodama

Míriam Lado
Alexandra Levenberg
Tino Martínez
Carlos Mayor
Johanna McKeon
Lindsey Meyers
Philippe de Montebello
Hanan Mounir
Ralph Müller
Victoriano Nodar
Juan Antonio Olañeta
Marta Oreiro
Mario R. Orlando
Emma Paterson
Fernando Pazó
Stefano Piantini
Natalia Pena
Juan Carlos Pichel
Blanca Prol
Silvia Riboldi
Ismail Serageldin
Nina Soufy
Esther Tallada
Sally Tingle
Ramón Villares
Sohair Wastawy
Josephine Watson
Claire Weatherhead